The Leading Edge of Safety

THE STORY OF SAFE FLIGHT INSTRUMENT CORPORATION

"I'm not interested in steering towards a known ending."

—Leonard Greene, Founder

The Leading Edge of Safety

THE STORY OF SAFE FLIGHT INSTRUMENT CORPORATION

by David Fisher

GREENWICH PUBLISHING GROUP, INC.

SAFE FLIGHT
INSTRUMENT CORPORATION

Produced and published by Greenwich Publishing Group, Inc.
Old Saybrook, Connecticut
www.greenwichpublishing.com

Designed by Clare Cunningham Graphic Design

Library of Congress Control Number: 2008940110

ISBN: 0-944641-73-3

First Printing: December 2008

10 9 8 7 6 5 4 3 2 1

Table of Contents

1: He Could See The Air

"He could see the air. I don't mean that as a metaphor. I mean it literally. He could visualize the flow and pressure of air in his mind."

—Randall Greene, President and CEO

I was the kind of day pilots dream of: a clear blue sky stretching beyond the horizon. An occasional puff of white cloud drifted lazily on a high wind, but near the ground there was barely a breeze. The year was 1937, and 19-year-old Leonard Greene was getting ready to take a flying lesson at the old U.S. Naval Air Station in Queens, New York, near the site of what is now John F. Kennedy International Airport. Greene was a chemist in his uncle's rubber cement company, but that was simply his day job. Flying was his passion—one that would last a lifetime.

Suddenly, with no warning and for seemingly no apparent reason, a small plane making an approach to the airport dropped out of the sky and slammed into the earth. People ran toward the crash site, but nothing could be done to save the pilot.

Greene stood there, watching and wondering: *why?*

In those early days of aviation, sudden death was a fact of life. Pilots knew the risks and accepted them as the price of their passion. Greene, however, was troubled by the crash. He couldn't simply accept it and walk away. While there was no way of knowing it at that time, that accident would change his life—and, along with it, the course of aviation safety.

SAMPLING THE WIND

As Leonard Greene later learned, the accident had been caused by an aerodynamic stall—a too common, often fatal occurrence in which an airplane rapidly loses its lift. To aeronautical engineers and pilots, a stall is the technical term defining the point at which the flow of air over the wings can no longer support the airplane's weight. The primary cause of a stall is not a lack of airspeed; it's a problem with the angle at which the wing cuts through the wind—the angle of attack. Air flowing around the wing supports an airplane in flight, and when the angle of attack exceeds a critical level, the lift the wing produces rapidly drops and can no longer support the plane's weight.

Pilots of the 1930s viewed stalling as an accepted risk. The fact was that before World War II nearly half of the nation's aviation accidents were caused by stalls. No one had been able to figure out how to prevent these accidents.

Leonard Greene may have been a chemist in a rubber cement company, but more than anything he was an inventor who loved to find solutions to seemingly impossible problems—and undetected wing stalls presented a serious problem that needed to be solved. He didn't set out to start a company. He wanted to solve a technical problem— one that cost lives.

The problem Greene faced was how to warn pilots that they were about to stall— before the stall actually occurred. He needed a device that would warn pilots that the plane was losing its lift, and to do that a sensor was needed to measure the wind angle at any speed. His solution: a short protruding vane positioned on the leading edge of the wing. Resembling a tongue sticking out of the wing, sampling the wind, it was connected to a microswitch. When the point was reached at which the flow of air separated into two streams—one above and one below the wing—and moved aft under the wing to a repeatable, critical point just before a stall would occur, the vane would move. That would close an electrical circuit, activate a horn and light on the cockpit instrument panel, and give the pilot a warning to adjust the airspeed and/or pitch attitude, keeping the plane in the air.

Greene built a rudimentary prototype. He called it, generically, a "stall warning system." It was, as Greene remembered, "a simplistic device with a sophisticated reason for working." Actually, it was an ingenious solution to a deadly problem.

Greene mounted the device on the leading edge of the wing of a fabric-covered

Fairchild 24 airplane and took off. "It worked," he explained years later. "It gave me exactly the result that I wanted. Just before the plane went into a stall, a horn went off and a light began flashing in the cockpit. The day after I invented it, I sent it off to the technical development division of the Civil Aeronautics Authority—the forerunner to the FAA—and then I went to work on something else."

No one could have imagined at that time that Leonard Greene's "simplistic device" would eventually be installed on nearly two-thirds of all the world's airplanes—an extraordinary level of success that made the stall warning system the foundation of Safe Flight Instrument Corporation, the world's oldest continuously operating avionics company. In the extraordinarily competitive aviation industry, where the companies of legendary pioneers like Elmer Sperry, Arthur Collins and Ed King eventually were absorbed or disappeared, Leonard Greene's Safe Flight continues to be the pioneer in lift instrumentation.

THE INVENTION OF THE STALL WARNING BEGAN WITH GREENE'S DISCOVERY THAT STALLS WERE CAUSED WHEN THE ANGLE OF ATTACK, THE ANGLE AT WHICH THE LEADING EDGE OF THE WING CUTS THROUGH THE AIR, GOT TOO STEEP. IF PILOTS WERE WARNED BEFORE THEY REACHED THAT CRITICAL POINT, HE BELIEVED, THEY COULD AVOID STALLS. GREENE RECALLED, "I MADE THE FIRST STALL WARNING IN THE NAVY AIRPORT OUT OF SCREW-DRIVERS AND BOLTS AND PIECES OF FLAT METAL. IT WAS POWERED BY A FLASHLIGHT BATTERY, AND THE WARNING SYSTEM WAS A BICYCLE HORN." AFTER WORLD WAR II, GREENE BEGAN PRODUC-ING RUDIMENTARY STALL WARN-INGS. TODAY A STALL WARNING DEVICE IS REQUIRED ON EVERY AIRPLANE—AND NEARLY TWO-THIRDS OF ALL AIRCRAFT CARRY SAFE FLIGHT PRODUCTS.

FLYING AHEAD OF THE AIRCRAFT

Leonard had the capacity to see beyond the obvious to find the often elusive answer to a problem, simple or complex. "His mind was always somewhere in the future," explains Senior Systems Design Engineer Peter Cordes, who worked closely with Leonard after coming to Safe Flight in 1963. "As a pilot, Leonard flew ahead of the aircraft. By the time he took off, he'd already figured out his landing. He knew what all the limitations were, he knew what his fuel reserves were, and he knew where all the storms were."

Growing up in the Roaring Twenties, Leonard was entranced by aviation. He built model airplanes and studied the maneuvers of World War I aerial combat pilots. He learned to fly at the age of 19—so long ago that his Civil Aeronautics Authority pilot's license had only five digits: 94271. He got a degree in chemical engineering from New York's City College and took a job at the family rubber cement and asbestos company. Rubber cement might have been his career—but for his love of aviation.

After attending New York University's Guggenheim School of Aeronautics, he went to work at Grumman Aircraft in theoretical aerodynamics and flight research. "I had the best job imaginable," he once recalled. "They gave me the run of five factories. I was free to work on anything that interested me, and Grumman gave me all the support I needed. I invented a helicopter with jets mounted on the tips of its rotors. I invented a 60-millimeter cannon shell that pierced wood without leaving a trace. I figured out a method that would enable American fighter planes, which were not as maneuverable as Japanese Zeros, to succeed against them in combat. And I wrote a paper proving it was possible to break the sound barrier."

FASTER THAN SOUND

Conventional thinking in the early part of the 20th century was that going faster than sound was a concept from science fiction, and most respected theoretical scientists believed it was impossible. But in 1943, Greene, then just 25 years old, wrote a paper entitled *The Attenuation Method for Compressible Flow Systems*. It not only accurately predicted what would happen when the sound barrier was broken, it also explained how to do it. Airplanes at that time had straight wings, so they literally met the air head on; Greene theorized that an angled wing, one swept toward the rear of the plane, would allow the wing to cut through air far more efficiently and, more importantly, delay the

What Makes a Stall?

SPEED? We've been taught that speed will always prevent a stall. This is not true. 80 mph may be perfectly safe under one condition but much too slow under other conditions. Sometimes we can feel it by the "seat of our pants", other times a stall can develop very quickly—even with plenty of speed and *even with the nose down. An airplane can be stalled at any speed.*

The SFI takes into account the effect of speed.

ACCELERATION? The G-load we put on the airplane actually determines the stalling speed more than anything else. A 2-G load, for instance, requires twice the lift and raises the stalling speed 42%. You can quickly raise the G-load not only in a steep turn but also by pulling back on the stick in any attitude. Gusty air also increases acceleration loads. Your normal flying involves a wide variation of G-loads.

The SFI takes into account the effect of acceleration

LOADING? Your stalling speed varies greatly with the load being carried. Full gas and a full load of passengers raises the landing speed, the safe approach speed and safe maneuvering speed.

The SFI takes into account the effect of load.

3

POWER? The amount of power makes a great amount of difference in the stalling attitude of the airplane and changes the speed at which it will stall.

The SFI takes into account the effect of power.

FLAPS? Some flaps merely increase drag, permit a steeper approach angle. Others increase lift and thereby lower the stalling speed. If flaps are suddenly raised, it is easy to stall out. Even the landing gear up or down can effect the stalling speed.

The SFI takes into account the effect of flaps.

ALTITUDE? High altitude or hot air will increase the stalling speed of an airplane. Pilots unaccustomed to high field operations are often fooled by this variation.

The SFI takes into account the effects of altitude.

No wonder even experi-

CONVINCING PILOTS ACCUSTOMED TO FLYING "BY THE SEAT OF THEIR PANTS" THAT THIS NEW DEVICE COULD SAVE THEIR LIVES REQUIRED GREENE TO EDUCATE THE AVIATION INDUSTRY. HE PUBLISHED THIS PROMOTIONAL BOOKLET AND TOOK IT WITH HIM TO MANY SMALL AIRPORTS. IT QUOTED HIS FRIEND, CELEBRITY AND WELL-KNOWN PRIVATE PILOT ARTHUR GODFREY, SAYING THAT THE DEVICE "SHOULD BE MADE MANDATORY." THE PHOTO OPPOSITE SHOWS A LIFT DETECTOR MOUNTED ON AN EARLY BEECHCRAFT BONANZA.

onset of Mach rise as a function of the wing-sweep angle. Leonard often used the analogy of a boxer's roundhouse punch, which comes from the side, as opposed to the much more powerful straight punch right to the nose.

Citing wartime security regulations, the government classified this paper—but Leonard always believed it was also classified to protect the reputations of the celebrated scientists who had written extensively that it was impossible to break the sound barrier.

It was on April 7, 1944, during a high-speed test flight of the F6F-3 Grumman Hellcat, that famed test pilot Corwin H. "Corky" Meyer unknowingly proved Leonard's thesis. As Meyer later wrote in his book *Corky Meyer's Flight Journal*:

"I pushed over from 28,000 feet to what I estimated to be a 60-degree dive angle.... With full power, the aircraft's descent rate soon built up to over 38,000 feet per minute. I estimated I would attain 485 mph indicated airspeed as I went through 10,000 feet and then make an easy two-and-a-half G pullout....

"Just before I was going to start the simple pullout I noticed with great alarm ... that the nose was going down fast of its own volition, rapidly increasing the dive angle and speed.... I was no longer flying, I was a passenger.... To counter this I began to pull the stick aft.... Nothing happened. So I pulled much harder.... The stick seemed to be stuck in concrete.... (S)omething way beyond my comprehension and capabilities was directing the aircraft straight into the ground. I had less than 10 seconds to live.

"I instinctively yanked the throttle from full power to the idle position and continued my two-handed pull on the stick, praying for recovery. (A)ll hell broke loose. The aircraft started buffeting violently and pulled up to 4Gs. My still frantic pull on the stick caused the Gs to continue to 7Gs with increasing buffeting.... The 7G pullout finally bottomed out at 2,500 feet altitude...."

As Meyer discovered, the only person at Grumman who could explain what had happened was Leonard Greene, whose theoretical paper, he wrote, "had described my predicament precisely." The airspeed achieved during the dive had caused the airflow to reach supersonic speeds, causing the wing's center of lift to move several feet back beyond its normal rear limit. "These effects had given the aircraft its strong buffeting, stuck-in-concrete stick elevator forces and pitch down," Meyer wrote. "[Greene]

WHILE MOST SCIENTISTS IN THE 1940s WERE CONFIDENT THAT THE SOUND BARRIER COULD NEVER BE BROKEN, LEONARD GREENE THOUGHT OTHERWISE. TEST PILOT CORKY MEYER PROVED HIM RIGHT IN 1944 DURING A FLIGHT IN A GRUMMAN HELLCAT SIMILAR TO THE F6F AT RIGHT. GREENE RECEIVED MANY AWARDS IN HIS LIFETIME, AMONG THEM, BELOW, THE 1949 *AVIATION WEEK* DISTINGUISHED SERVICE AWARD.

continued by stating that my closing the throttle greatly increased the aircraft drag and that, coupled with the normal increase of the speed of sound with decreasing altitude, had reduced my Mach number sufficiently to back the aircraft out of its critical shock wave compressibility condition. With the center of lift again restored to its proper place, normal stick forces were instantly available...."

Meyer later wrote a letter to Leonard. He said, "As I remember, you once gave me a dissertation on the compressibility effects of the Hellcat and were right on the button when all other Grummanites were looking with awed consternation at the unpredictable problems relative to high speeds in the Hellcat. That information stood me in great stead during the following years. I thank you again for your words of wisdom in April of 1943."

Leonard Greene's ability to understand this complex situation and its resolution came from an extraordinary gift, his son, Safe Flight President and CEO Randall Greene, says. "He could see the air. I don't mean that as a metaphor. I mean it literally. He could visualize the flow of pressure and air in his mind. He could imagine any shape moving through air or water at any speed and evaluate its flow field."

ATTITUDE IS NOT ANGLE-OF-ATTACK

ATTITUDE 180°
ANGLE-OF-ATTACK 3°

ATTITUDE 270°   ATTITUDE 90°
ANGLE-OF-ATTACK 3°   ANGLE-OF-ATTACK 3°

ATTITUDE 0°
ANGLE-OF-ATTACK 3°

WING CHORD
RELATIVE WIND

In addition to laying the basis for an understanding of the pressures exerted by aerodynamic forces at supersonic speeds, Greene's paper had an impact that reverberated through aviation history.

GOING INTO PRODUCTION

Leonard Greene had spent World War II inventing a part of aviation's future, but at the end of the war he had to decide what his own future would be. He recalled that "there were two things I wanted to do: either manufacture my stall warning system or become a professor of aeronautics. Both paths appealed equally to me, but finally I decided to break with theory and go into production."

For the cash he needed to start his company, Greene borrowed money from his mother, bought a Fairchild 24 Ranger from his friend, future IBM Chief Executive Thomas J. Watson Jr., and opened an air taxi service. His passengers included Watson; legendary

golfer Sam Snead; Katherine Reynolds, the wife of tobacco baron R. J. Reynolds; Amory Houghton, president of Corning Glass Company, and bandleader Guy Lombardo. By October 1946, he'd raised enough money to rent a drafty old wooden barn—large enough for about two horses—on Russell Street in White Plains, New York. The rent was $100 a month. He hired a woman named Lottie Ehlers for $25 a week, bought an old drill press, and opened his business.

Leonard named his company Safe Flight, the somewhat optimistic name he'd used for his air taxi service. It came from a slogan he'd seen years earlier on a matchbook cover: *Have A Light, Have A Safe Flight.*

At first there were few buyers for Safe Flight's innovative Stall Warning Indicator. At $17, the device's price tag was a lot of money in those days, especially for new, unproven technology. Greene survived for several months by cutting up long aluminum rods and making antennas for the latest invention then sweeping the nation: television. He even climbed roofs and installed them for his customers.

Eventually, though, Greene was able to convince the chief engineer of the Arrow Insurance Underwriters Company to offer a 3 percent discount on aircraft hull insurance to anyone who installed a stall warning system in his plane—a promotional gimmick that also made economic sense. (That same hull insurance discount strategy is used today to market Safe Flight's helicopter powerline detection system.) As Greene recalled, "Safe Flight became a business on the day we made more stall warning indicators than TV antennas. But even then, for a long time, it was a business of nickels and dimes."

By 1948 pilots were praising Leonard's invention. *The Saturday Evening Post* called it "the greatest life saver since the invention of the parachute." It is impossible to estimate how many thousands of lives the Stall Warning Indicator has saved, but as Greene noted, "Eventually stalls went from being the worst cause of airplane accidents to almost no cause at all."

As orders finally started to come in, Greene began hiring new workers. Within two

SAFE FLIGHT'S FIRST OFFICE OPENED IN 1946 IN THIS BARN, HOUSING LEONARD, ANOTHER EMPLOYEE, AND AN OLD DRILL PRESS. BY 1950 THERE WERE SIX EMPLOYEES, OPPOSITE, PUTTING A STRAIN ON THE STRUCTURE. AFTER THE FLOOR CRACKED IN 1951, SAFE FLIGHT MOVED INTO THE SECOND FLOOR OF A BRICK GARAGE. THE COMPANY CONSTRUCTED ITS OWN BUILDING NEAR WHITE PLAINS AIRPORT IN 1964 AND, THROUGH SEVERAL EXPANSIONS, HAS BEEN THERE EVER SINCE.

Many owners report..."It paid for itself...and pays us a steady profit!"

new 1948 Stinson Flying Station Wagon

years, Safe Flight had grown to six employees, about as many as could work together in the former barn on Russell Street. From the day he opened the barn door for business, Greene set out to establish a very different kind of corporate culture, a company with a uniquely close relationship between management and labor. "My first problem was how to develop an innovative employee plan to ensure that we could recruit and then keep high-quality personnel," he said. "The solution was a comprehensive—and at that time, innovative—benefits package, as well as a working structure that was loose enough to ensure production, one that would encourage creativity and would foster strong working relationships."

SAFE FLIGHT TOOK OFF AFTER AN INSURER OFFERED A DISCOUNT TO AIRCRAFT OWNERS WHO INSTALLED STALL WARNINGS. IN 1948 CONSOLIDATED VULTEE MADE SAFE FLIGHT'S DEVICE STANDARD EQUIPMENT ON ITS STINSON VOYAGER AND, SHOWN IN THE AD ABOVE, FLYING STATION WAGON MODELS.

The impact of the benefits plan that Leonard offered paid off. Employees came to work at Safe Flight and stayed. And stayed. Some have now been with the company for nearly 50 years.

THE 35-CENT LUNCH

In the early days, Leonard and his first sales manager, Marvin Waldman, would fly from airport to airport demonstrating and selling the Stall Warning Indicator, often visiting as many as three airports a day. An airport manager could become an "official Safe Flight dealer" by purchasing three stall warning systems. In 1948 Consolidated Vultee Aircraft Corporation of Wayne, Michigan, became the first company to make the Stall Warning Indicator standard equipment on new airplanes, installing it on its four-seat Stinson 165 Voyager and Flying Station Wagon models.

Almost immediately Leonard began making improvements to his warning system. In 1949 he added a "stick shaker," an off-center weight driven by a small electric motor that would cause the steering stick to vibrate—similar to the natural buffet effect of an aerodynamic wing stall. The stick shaker met with immediate success, ensuring the continued existence of Safe Flight. "There was a diner on the corner," Leonard recalled. "I'd go there every day for the 25-cent lunch, which was all I could afford. But on the day Grumman ordered 100 of our stick shakers, I went into that diner and told the waitress, 'Today I'll have the 35-cent lunch—the one with meat!' When we got that order from Grumman, I knew we were going to make it."

The key to the success of the Stall Warning Indicator lay in its wing leading-edge detector, the vane sticking into the wind. By 1951 Safe Flight had expanded on that basic vane microswitch with an analog vane position transducer, making it capable of measuring a range of wing leading-edge airflow positions, thus providing vital information that became the foundation of later Safe Flight products.

To function properly, the transducer had to be installed at a very specific point on the wing, the position that would give the precise measurement of the airflow at performance-critical speeds at high angles of attack. Because every model of aircraft was different, that point had to be identified on every type of plane. "It was like putting your finger on the pulse of the airplane," Leonard explained. "It was the center of the operation, and with the data we could get from that point, there were endless things we could do."

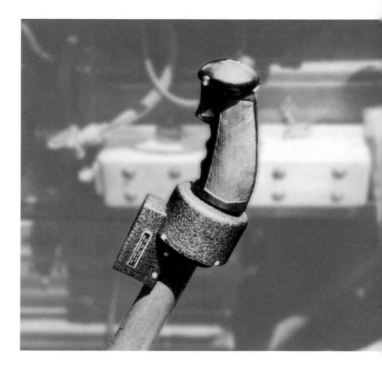

A STICK SHAKER WAS ADDED TO SAFE FLIGHT'S STALL WARNING SYSTEM IN 1949 TO ELIMINATE ANY POSSIBLE CONFUSION IN THE COCKPIT ABOUT THE MEANING OF A LIGHT OR HORN AND TO SIMULATE THE BUFFET OF AN AERODYNAMIC STALL. IT WAS AN UNMISTAKABLE WARNING TO A PILOT THAT THE AIRCRAFT WAS ABOUT TO STALL.

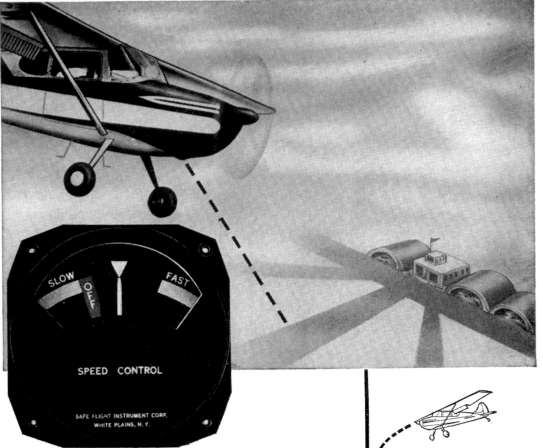

PRECISION APPROACH SPEED NOW INSURED WITH

SAFE FLIGHT

SPEED CONTROL SYSTEM

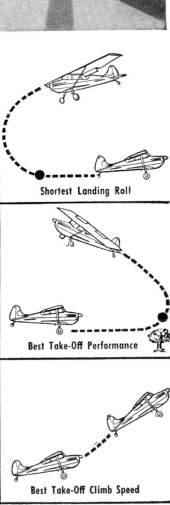

Shortest Landing Roll

Best Take-Off Performance

Best Take-Off Climb Speed

Pilots are unanimous in their approval of the new Safe Flight Speed Control System that "takes the mathematics out of precision approaches, landings and take-offs" and substitutes all-inclusive, *instantaneous lift instrumentation.*

The Safe Flight Speed Control System computes for power, gross weight, maneuvering, turbulence, etc., activating the pointer on a single standard instrument panel dial. With pointer centered, speed and attitude are correct, regardless of airspeed readings. Maintaining proper wing lift condition becomes a simple matter of pitch and/or throttle control! Readings are continuous, all-inclusive, non-lagging. Data is gathered instantly from a wing-mounted lift transducer (de-icer-protected for multi-engine planes).

AVAILABLE FOR SINGLE (MODEL SC-12) AND MULTI-ENGINE AIRCRAFT (MODEL SC-24)

Ask your dealer, or write or wire for
detailed information, stating type aircraft.

SAFE FLIGHT INSTRUMENT CORPORATION

"Pioneers in Lift Instrumentation"

Over the next 60 years, Safe Flight's engineers would combine the rudimentary stall warning system with an array of other inputs, such as wing flap position, longitudinal and normal acceleration, pitch angle and rates, and aircraft configuration, to develop an array of products that make flying safer and more economical: devices known as "stick pushers" that help pilots automatically recover from a stall condition; analog and digital angle of attack systems that enable pilots to fly both safely and optimally for range and endurance; automatic throttle controls that control the speed of the aircraft from takeoff to touchdown; an altitude alert system; instrument panel vibrators; takeoff and go-around computers; pitch guidance systems; landing and approach indicators; and a wind shear detector.

"The person who sits in the back of one of our aircraft just assumes our airplane is going to be safe," says Joe Lombardo, president of Gulfstream Aerospace Corporation, a Safe Flight customer since the mid-1950s, when the Gulfstream I was introduced. "That assumption isn't just based on blind faith, it's based on a historical record for safety. That's a major discriminator when customers buy one of our products; they know reliability and safety are part of our history. So when we purchase products from Safe Flight, they have to meet a very high standard to fulfill our customers' expectations."

Safe Flight products are on every Gulfstream airplane. According to Gulfstream's president emeritus, Bryan Moss, "From the start, there were technical capabilities and a work attitude at Safe Flight that appealed to Gulfstream. The fact that the relationship has continued for such a long period of time is good evidence that Safe Flight is doing the right things in terms of technology, quality, and reliability."

More than 400 variations of Safe Flight's basic lift detector and lift transducers have been developed, many of them still in use. The company has sold more than a half million lift detectors and lift transducers, and it dominates the leading-edge detection market. Leonard Greene's original $17 device—built on an obsession to solve a problem and save lives—has grown into sophisticated stall warning systems that are found on the entire spectrum of the world's aircraft, from small fixed-wing planes to the most advanced commercial and military jets.

FIFTY YEARS AFTER SAFE FLIGHT INTRODUCED ITS STALL WARNING, BELOW, THE OWNER OF A PRIVATE PLANE WITH AN ORIGINAL SYSTEM REQUESTED A NEW LENS FOR ITS WARNING LAMP. SAFE FLIGHT WAS ABLE TO REPLACE THE LENS, AND THE SYSTEM CONTINUED IN USE. SAFE FLIGHT HAS PRODUCED MORE THAN 400 VARIATIONS OF THE DEVICE FOR ALL TYPES OF AIRCRAFT.

2: The Problem Solvers

As a small company competing against large corporations, Safe Flight had to rely from the beginning on innovation, technical excellence, and production quality.

By the late 1940s it had become clear that, if Safe Flight was going to succeed, it needed room to grow. The industry's response to the company's stall warning indicators demanded more space for a growing workforce to build the devices—as well as to invent, develop, and manufacture new products. In 1950 Leonard Greene finally got the message that Safe Flight had outgrown its barn when the plank floor cracked under the weight of a heavy drill press.

Leonard responded by leasing the entire second floor of a brick building, above a roofing and gutter installation company, at 4 Water Street in White Plains. The raw space was partitioned into appropriate departments, each a bit cramped. The building had no air conditioning and little heat. In the summer the office got so hot that employees would spray water from garden hoses on the metal roof to cool it down. In the winter it was so cold that employees couldn't start the workday until the building finally got up to temperature around 10 a.m.; even then, they sometimes had to wear gloves and woolen caps. Maintenance Supervisor Sam Cambriello remembers sitting down in the boiler room all day—and on occasion through the night—feeding water into the ancient, slightly cracked boiler to keep it going.

FIRST EMPLOYEES

Ralph Friedman and Bill Schmitt were among Safe Flight's first employees. Friedman was an aeronautical engineer who started in the drafting department in 1949 and rapidly worked his way up to become Safe Flight's first executive vice president. Greene and Friedman were a team, with Ralph as Leonard's right-hand man. With a smile and a few nice words, he made sure that just about everything that Leonard needed got done— from getting salaries paid every Thursday to shepherding Leonard's ideas into product development to staying with the Greenes' children when Leonard was away.

"Ralph was basically Leonard's eyes and ears," explains Joe Gordon, senior vice president of engineering. "He made it his business to be on a first-name basis with each employee." Adds Bill McIntosh of the production department, "Ralph Friedman had the whole business in his head. Every unit we made, every component, he knew everything about it. But he also knew people's birthdays and their children's names and what was in the storage room. We used to say that Ralph worked here 24 hours a day."

Another early employee was Bill Schmitt, who exemplified the type of worker Leonard Greene liked to hire. When he began working at Safe Flight in 1949, Schmitt was a non-skilled employee with a strong work ethic and a willingness to learn—and he was physically challenged, having lost a leg in World War II's Battle of the Bulge.

Schmitt ultimately worked at Safe Flight for 25 years and in 1966 was joined by his son, Dick, who entered the company as an assembler and who later became the plant manager.

Like most children of Safe Flight's employees, Dick Schmitt had often visited the plant while growing up and had attended many of the family picnics and Christmas parties. "Leonard always wanted to help the little guy," Dick remembers warmly. "He was always looking for people who needed a break—like my father." Safe Flight is the only place Dick Schmitt has worked in his career, and his presence at Safe Flight means that a Schmitt has been showing up for work there nearly every morning for almost 60 years.

Other employees have brought members of their families into the company, too. The three Banks brothers—John, Henry, and Bobby—combine for a total of 69 years of service. Production Manager Greg Tassio met his wife, Marisal, and engineer Paul Levine met his wife, Mary Lou, at Safe Flight. "For a long time, I did my best to ignore her, " Levine says of Mary Lou. "Until she left for another job. Then I realized how much I missed her."

THE FIRST SPIN-OFF PRODUCTS

As a small company competing against large aviation corporations, Safe Flight had to rely from the very beginning on innovation, technical excellence, and production quality to build and maintain a reputation. Customers had to know when they purchased a Safe Flight product that they could rely on it.

ACCESS TO THE WATER STREET BUILDING'S UPPER FLOOR, ABOVE, WAS BY A LONG RAMP ON THE SIDE, AND ON SNOWY DAYS IT HAD TO BE SHOVELED BEFORE WORK COULD BEGIN. MOST OF THE STAFF STANDS ON THAT RAMP, OPPOSITE, IN THIS LATE 1950s PHOTOGRAPH. STANDING NEXT TO LEONARD GREENE, FRONT ROW CENTER, IS RALPH FRIEDMAN, WHO WOULD LATER BECOME EXECUTIVE VICE PRESIDENT.

PRODUCT DEVELOPMENT WITH LEONARD

In the early days, every Safe Flight product began as Leonard Greene's idea. When he had a concept he wanted to discuss, he'd drag as many people as possible into his office. While these conscripts usually worked in engineering or design, sometimes the group included people from maintenance or assembly—and, on one occasion, a complete stranger.

Norm Rosenblum, manager of international contracts, remembers the afternoon in 1985 he came to Safe Flight to interview for a job. "I was just standing there, and Leonard invited me into his office where a meeting was about to begin. I didn't know who he was, and he certainly had no idea who I was. But I remember his enthusiasm. I sat down and listened as three people made a presentation about creative ways to finance a new and expensive project.

"Eventually the three men left, and I was still sitting there, along with several Safe Flight employees who also had no idea who I was but who didn't seem surprised that a stranger was there. Leonard began discussing the proposal with these men. Then he turned to me and asked me for my opinion. When I answered, he paid attention. He made me part of the decision-making process, and I didn't even work there."

Usually when Leonard called a meeting, no one had any idea what the subject might be. "We'd always begin these meetings the same way," remembers engineer Paul Levine, who worked with Leonard to develop many of his inventions. "We'd begin with Leonard explaining his idea, then I would

tell him why it was impossible. And then he would prove to me that it could work, and we'd go around and around until we came up with a result that would work."

Although Leonard Greene passed away in November 2006, his creative legacy lives on in many forms, among them an important future Safe Flight product. It's a multi-function air data probe that combines information from angle of attack sensors, Pitot probe, and static ports into a single unit. "That was Leonard's concept. He kicked it off at a meeting in his house less than a year before his death," says Vice President of Research and Development Robert Teter. "Traditionally, we had to punch three holes in the aircraft to do what this one multi-function probe will accomplish. We believe this is a product that will be successful for a long time in the future."

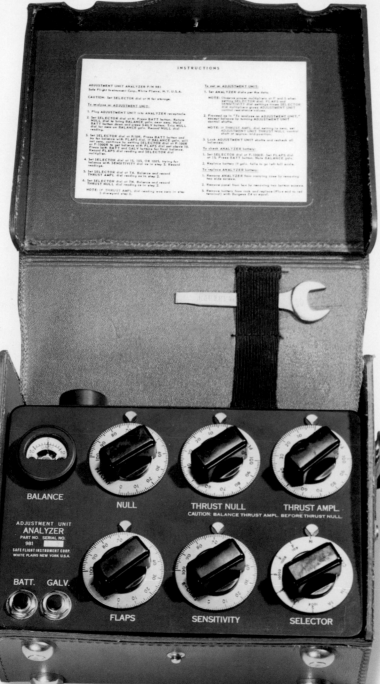

LEONARD GREENE, AT BENCH,

OPPOSITE, AND RALPH FRIEDMAN,

TO HIS LEFT, KNEW EVERY DETAIL

OF EVERY PROJECT. THE BOY IS

RANDALL GREENE, LEONARD'S SON

AND SAFE FLIGHT'S CURRENT CEO.

THE MID-1950s ANALYZER AT LEFT

WAS AMONG THE TOOLS USED TO

DEVELOP AN EARLY AUTOPOWER

SYSTEM.

The quality of the Stall Warning Indicator was high, and demand for the device was so strong that Safe Flight's workforce spilled out of its new building—the engineering department and model shop moving into space on the second floor of Hangar D at nearby Westchester County Airport. Leonard, meanwhile, was at work conceiving new products based on the core technology of the Stall Warning Indicator and the key angle of attack information it provided.

Leonard knew that there are basically two ways to fly an airplane—by airspeed or by angle of attack (AoA). Most pilots were trained to depend on their airspeed to make vital flight decisions, but Leonard believed angle of attack to be a far better—and safer—way to fly. There are several reasons for this. First, the recommended airspeed for specific segments of a flight changes with the weight of the airplane, while the angle of attack remains constant. Furthermore, there is an inherent delay in indicated airspeed—a perilous amount of time if a pilot encounters a wind shear, for example—while changes in the angle of attack register almost instantly. Finally, the angle of attack as sensed by Safe Flight's lift transducer provides information a pilot would otherwise have to obtain from three or four other instruments, making the job of flying considerably more efficient. As Joe Gordon explains, "Angle of attack is the better mousetrap. It's not the only way of catching mice, but it's a better way than most people have been taught."

To demonstrate the advantage of flying angle of attack, in 2005 Randall Greene flew Safe Flight's AoA indicator, combined with Safe Flight's automatic throttle system, coast-to-coast on Safe Flight's Falcon 20F-5, conserving enough fuel to enable him to make a nonstop flight from White Plains to San Diego in a headwind that averaged more than 100 miles per hour in a record six hours and 41 minutes.

Having the wing lift transducer in place to measure the airflow angle as it divides at the wing's leading edge made it possible for Safe Flight to create new products using that information. One of the first was a manually flown speed control system to help Navy pilots land their planes on aircraft carrier decks. At this time, the Navy was the only military service that taught its pilots to fly by angle of attack rather than airspeed, so it was the perfect place to develop this technology. The speed control system output drove three colored lights on the leading edge of the plane's wing to give the landing signal officer on the carrier deck the ability to judge an approaching plane's angle of attack and thus give the pilot guidance for the most precise touchdown at the proper speed.

In 1951 Leonard cruised on the USS *Midway* during the product's testing and evaluation phase. As a result of those tests, Safe Flight received its first significant order from the Navy, establishing a relationship with U.S. government programs that has continued for half a century, through numerous products and involving all branches of the military service.

THE SCAT COMPUTER

Throughout Safe Flight's history, most of its new products were built on the foundation of successful products that preceded them. Says Randall Greene, "That's what we do as a core practice: find new ways to expand on the technology we've created for the aviation industry."

Safe Flight's initial development of the Speed Command of Attitude and Thrust (SCAT) computer in 1958 was a perfect example. Before SCAT, pilots had to continually monitor several instruments during takeoff and landing and integrate the information from each of them into a set of pitch attitude adjustments and thrust changes to ensure a precise takeoff or landing. They had only a few seconds to do it, and if they encountered a problem with any aspect of the plane's performance or with weather conditions, they had only "raw" data to fly by.

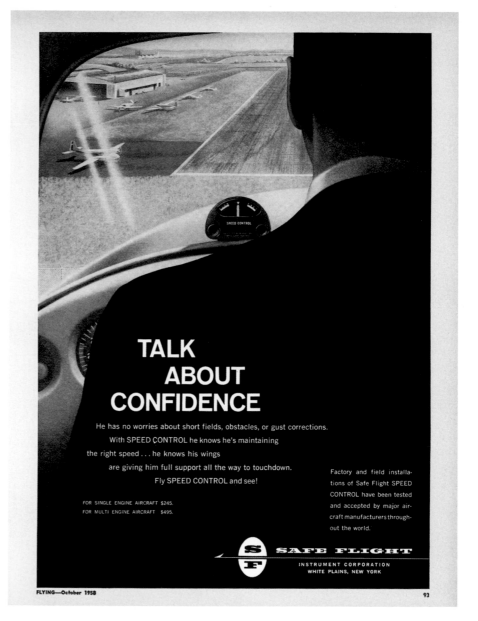

SCAT represented a new concept in avionics. It took information—such as the plane's longitudinal acceleration, wing flap configuration, landing gear position, outside air temperature, etc.—and combined it with angle of attack data from the Safe Flight transducer. It then generated a pitch command signal displayed on the flight director pitch command bar for takeoff and go-around pitch attitude guidance and a similar thrust command, on the fast/slow indicator, which would reliably guide pilots to fly the optimum pitch attitude or thrust requirement for safety and performance—under all conditions. Pilots needed to look at only one integrated display instead of several flight instruments. If the pilot kept the pitch command and fast/slow indicator centered, the

computer would direct the necessary pitch attitude and thrust adjustments, and the plane would fly at the correct angle of attack, yielding a stable, flight-profile-optimized takeoff, landing, or go-around.

Safe Flight installed SCAT on its Beechcraft Twin Bonanza during development. "The concept worked right away. The hardware didn't," remembered Sid Kraft, project engineer. "A whole bunch of parameters had to be tweaked. Leonard would pilot the test flights; he was able to change the numbers in his head as if the circuit was changing them, so he could do things to compensate for what the hardware didn't do. And then we would put it in the hardware so pilots wouldn't have to compensate for it."

Allegheny Airlines, the predecessor to US Airways and the first commercial airline to put SCAT into service, was so taken with SCAT's capabilities that it even produced literature to explain the system's uniqueness to passengers: "While most instruments in the aircraft's cockpit respond to existing conditions, indicating to the pilot that a situation exists after it has already been created, the SCAT system is so ingenious it actually anticipates what will happen, based on little bits and pieces of information fed to it automatically. This permits the pilot to take action before a situation exists."

Bearing in mind the power of today's computers, consider that in the late 1950s there were no computers at all—only rudimentary calculating machines, able to handle a limited number of analog computations. Transistors didn't exist either, so SCAT used large magnetic amplifiers to amplify electrical signals. The result was that SCAT took the physical form of a big box that had to fit into already crowded avionics compartments on every different airplane model.

By 1959 the U.S. military had put SCAT into regular service, installing it on the Douglas C-9A/B, the Air Force and Navy military version of the DC-9. Within two years Boeing, Convair, and Lockheed had purchased systems, and SCAT was being used by more than 24 airlines around the world. SCAT proved to be a very successful Safe Flight product for more than a decade, with 3,500 systems produced and installed.

Eventually SCAT fell victim to its own success and the evolution of technology. Safe Flight's larger competitors began bundling their own competing pitch and thrust command systems, creating the integrated flight deck—and making certain there was no space available for stand-alone products such as SCAT. Though the market for SCAT as a stand-alone system gradually diminished, as a subcontractor, Safe Flight has

THE INDICATOR FOR SAFE FLIGHT'S SPEED CONTROL SYSTEM IS INSTALLED, OPPOSITE, IN THE COMPANY'S 1957 BEECHCRAFT BONANZA V35J. BELOW ARE SAFE FLIGHT'S C-50 AND D-50 TWIN BONANZAS FROM THE 1960s. ABOVE, A MODEL DISPLAYS THE SCAT COMPUTER IN AN ALLEGHENY AIRLINES ADVERTISEMENT PROMOTING A COMMITMENT TO PASSENGER SAFETY.

SAFE FLIGHT'S LONG AND SUC-
CESSFUL RELATIONSHIP WITH THE
MILITARY BEGAN IN 1951 WHEN
THE NAVY, WHOSE PILOTS FLY
ANGLE OF ATTACK, PLACED THE
FIRST LARGE ORDER FOR STALL
WARNING SYSTEMS—REQUESTING
THAT THEY BE DESIGNED FOR USE
IN AIRCRAFT CARRIER LANDINGS.
LEONARD GREENE SAILED ABOARD
THE USS *MIDWAY* TO TEST THE
SYSTEM THAT ENABLED LANDING
SIGNAL OFFICERS TO DETERMINE
THE PRECISION OF A PILOT'S
APPROACH. SAFE FLIGHT HAS
SINCE WORKED WITH ALL
BRANCHES OF THE U.S. MILITARY,
AS WELL AS THE MILITARIES OF
MANY OTHER COUNTRIES, ON A
VARIETY OF COMBAT AND CARGO
AIRPLANES. THE RELATIONSHIP
RECENTLY EXTENDED TO HELICOP-
TERS, AS BOTH THE ARMY AND
NAVY INSTALLED SAFE FLIGHT'S
HELICOPTER EXCEEDANCE
WARNING SYSTEM.

provided SCAT and other products to competitors for inclusion in their integrated cockpits.

Development and refinement of SCAT has continued through the years, however. Among the added capabilities is RRG (Runway Rotation Guidance), which basically tells the pilot when to lift off—based on a comparison of inertial acceleration with airspeed acceleration. The adaptation of new computer technology has made SCAT considerably smaller and more powerful. A modern version with a digital interface is one of the key products Safe Flight provides for the Boeing/U.S. Air Force fleet of RC-135 reconnaissance aircraft today.

THE FIRST CRUISE CONTROL IN THE SKY

Even before Safe Flight's SCAT computer had been adopted throughout the commercial aviation industry, the company was already planning enhancements to make it even more valuable to pilots. The first substantial addition was an automatic throttle system known as AutoPower. Essentially an aeronautical "cruise control," AutoPower works in conjunction with SCAT to control the aircraft to a pilot-selected indicated airspeed or Mach number while providing angle of attack protection throughout the flight.

The concept was a simple one: maintaining the desired speed during an approach usually resulted in an accurate landing, but on occasion, conditions such as turbulence and/or wind shear made manually adhering to the target speed difficult, and coming in too fast or too slow made it almost impossible to hit the desired touchdown point. The automatic throttle system that Safe Flight developed offered pilots consistency and safety in landing their aircraft—allowing them to touch down consistently on every landing. Once the pilot set a target speed, AutoPower controlled the throttles to maintain it.

The concept of an aircraft cruise control system was new, and AutoPower became the first proven speed management system.

"TURN THE SO-AND-SO"

Safe Flight developed the original AutoPower system in cooperation with Trans World Airlines. TWA Chief Pilot Gordy Granger was looking for a way to improve the accuracy of his pilots' touchdown points. TWA had its own engineering department, capable of analyzing sophisticated instrumentation on its own, and the company approached Safe Flight to work jointly on this project.

The development process was long and often tedious. A group of Safe Flight engineers practically lived in a motel near TWA's Kansas City headquarters. "We put one of the first boxes on a TWA 707 and flight-tested it," Joe Gordon recalls. "Things weren't going very well. It wouldn't work consistently. We were dealing with pitch rates and dynamic maneuvers, trying to get the maneuver to work smoothly with the autopilot, and sometimes it worked perfectly and other times it didn't. We continued to try different adjustments, but we were having a hard time. Things weren't going our way. The flight test was nearing an end, and we were really frustrated. At Leonard's beckoning, I was making adjustments. Finally, he told me, 'Well, turn the so-and-so.'

"I asked him, 'Which part?'

"Half-kidding, he said, 'Every knob.' We kept at it and we kept at it. We changed things and redesigned things, and eventually we got it right. One thing about Safe Flight: we are persistent. We keep working until we get it right—and we did. We got it absolutely right. It worked beautifully, and it was a great product."

TWA installed SCAT and AutoPower on every airplane in its fleet.

Douglas Aircraft soon grew interested in AutoPower for its new DC-9. Leonard was scheduled to demonstrate the system to a group of Douglas engineers and test pilots, but the system wasn't quite ready. He and Flight Test Engineer Ed Johnson flew Safe Flight's Beechcraft Twin Bonanza from White Plains,

New York, to Long Beach, California, for a demonstration. Johnson spent most of the 15-hour, cross-country flight cramped in the baggage compartment, huddled over the computer, making adjustments as Leonard shouted information to him. Douglas bought the system for the DC-9, and Safe Flight opened a satellite operations center in Long Beach to install and support the system.

In the late 1960s the Federal Aviation Agency issued new air traffic control regulations requiring commercial pilots to fly at certain speeds during different portions of a landing approach. In its original version, AutoPower controlled only angle of attack and didn't include a variable airspeed select function, so it couldn't adjust to those mandated speeds. Swissair approached Safe Flight and asked the company to find a way to make the system work on its DC-9s, factoring in the new speed control requirements. In response, Safe Flight made the first of many major revisions to the autothrottle system: adding an airspeed select controller that enabled a pilot to manually select an airspeed.

TESTING THE B-47

The B-47 Stratojet was a breakthrough, swept-wing jet bomber that became the mainstay of the Strategic Air Command's fleet during the early Cold War years. The plane—which had six engines—was so fast that, in 1948, test pilot Chuck Yeager couldn't keep up with a prototype B-47 while chasing it in a Lockheed P-80 jet fighter. Because the B-47 had a reputation for being fast on landings, the U.S. Air Force evaluated Safe Flight's Landing Speed Indicator for the airplane. Leonard Greene conducted the test flights, serving as navigator on a three-man crew. He wrote this reminiscence in his diary shortly after the first successful test flights in the early 1950s.

We got here. Here was Wright-Patterson Air Force Base, where Uncle Sam had just placed $15 million worth of airplanes at my disposal—three B-47 jet bombers. The purpose of this mission was to go up in these monsters and see if the Safe Flight Landing Speed Indicator worked. If it did, we were going to be able to land these enormous machines at three times an express train's speed within the 1½ -mile airport. If not, ….

First came the wearing apparel. Along with the parachute was supplied a crash helmet, sewn-in oxygen tank, regulators, gauges, microphone, earphones, electric blanket, shoulder harness, crash belt, first aid kit, sun shade, and a can opener (I was suspicious of the can opener). The preflight briefing consisted of instructions on how to bail out of the airplane. If the emergency siren wails three times, you pull the emergency cabin depressurizer, pull the emergency air lock door, pull the emergency exit wind flap screen, fasten the emergency oxygen bottle, unfasten the emergency parachute, release, and jump. At this point, the copilot muttered to me, "Not me, brother. In testing the bail-out system, every dummy they tried to parachute out of this plane in order to test the egress system had its head sheared off by being blown against the tail. I recommend you crawl behind the seat and cover your face. I'm using the can opener."

I was briefed and ready to go. Just then, the fire engines came wailing up. *Miss B-47* had caught on fire. After the commotion was over, I discovered that there is an electrical power box that had enough current to light a city. It had short-circuited. So, on to the next B-47. This girl was more agreeable. We even managed to get the engines started. Then one of the 2,536,721 switches decided not to work. The crew chief came on board. *Miss B-47* liked the crew chief, and when he pressed the switch, she purred.

The takeoff was a thrill that only a B-47 can give. Faster, faster, faster,

faster … but the airplane did not leave the runway. I looked at the airspeed indicator. We were going 200 miles per hour—more than the top speed of most commercial airplanes—and we hadn't left the ground! However, just as the end of the runway appeared, we started to fly.

Reluctant as our girl was to leave the ground, once airborne, she climbed like she was weightless. The altimeter raced around too fast to follow, and in a moment we were high above the clouds, going 600 miles an hour in an absolute space-type stillness. I cannot describe it, except to say that, if there is a sitting on top of the world, this was it.

Now came the acid test. Here was a little pipsqueak of an instrument, our Safe Flight Indicator, nestling amidst millions of dollars of computers, radars, gyroscopes, barometers, gauges, electronics, and super-electronics. Would it work? Could Safe Flight be right and Sperry, Bendix, Kollsman, Minneapolis Honeywell, and half of Wall Street be wrong? I set up the instrument, said I was ready, and told the pilot, Colonel Walters, to land. I knocked on wood six times: three times for the instrument and three times for Mrs. Greene's husband.

We came in for the landing. The speed was enormous, *Miss B-47* was enormous, and the airport suddenly started to shrink and shrink and shrink. Just when it was ready to disappear entirely, the power went on again. Colonel Walters decided not to land for fear of not stopping. We tried it again. This time, we made it but with not too much to spare. When I got out, Colonel Walters said that he didn't use our Landing Speed Indicator for the first landing attempt because he didn't trust it. But he did on the second, and it got us in safely!

How relieved I was that I was all finished. I was ready for a quick trip home for dinner, a bath, and bed. But *Miss B-47* wasn't through with me yet.

Upon landing, I found out that the first B-47 was almost fixed and that I was scheduled to align the indicator in it at 9:00 the next morning.

I didn't sleep too well. The next morning, I led myself back with trepidations. I strapped on my emergency gear and got into the bomber's seat while the jets were being fired up. Between the $250,000 radar bombing computer and the side of the fuselage was wedged a comic book left by my predecessor. He didn't worry about life insurance before each trip.

We were set to take off when I got a strong smell of burning rubber. Out of a hole in the complex bombing gear, smoke had started to pour. I shouted into the radio, "Fire!" and scrambled out. We abandoned the ship to the fire crew. Once more, I was set for home, bath, and bed, but—oh, no—*Miss B-47* still wasn't finished. They got the fire out, found the faulty circuit, and again we were ready to fly. This time, she got off.

Heaven again, or the nearest thing to it—sitting in a plastic bubble, noiselessly speeding at 600 mph above some messy snowstorms. I followed the same procedure: set up the indicator and came in for a landing. Again the airport wasn't large enough, and the decision was made to go around. The power was applied. There was a lurch, and we started to turn left. Two of the left engines had quit. The treetops were just below us, and the airplane was on the brink of turning over. The remaining four engines groaned and groaned and groaned. The pilot sweated, the copilot sweated.

I know what I did.

No, I am not dead. I am sitting in my nice, safe, comfortable, 200-mph Beech Bonanza, writing this story and singing to myself, "Home, dinner, bath, bed."

Goodbye, *Miss B-47*.

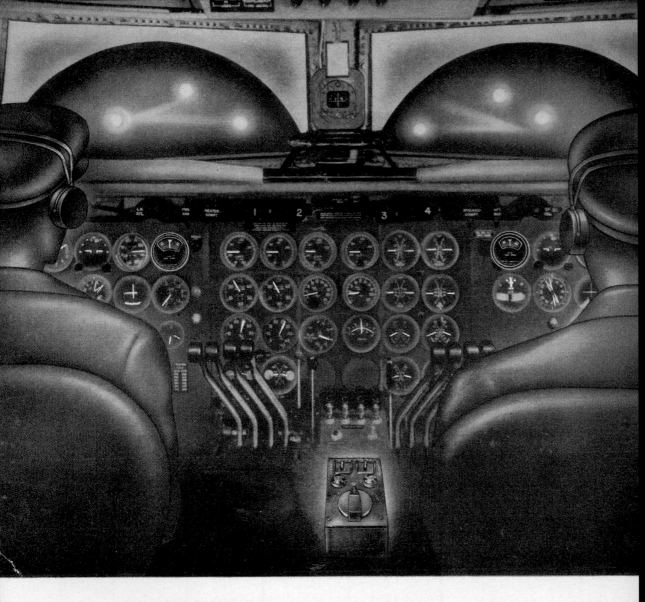

AUTOPOWER*

controls the fourth flight dimension <u>automatically</u>

Control of the airplane's glide path during landing approaches is divided between power and elevator. With AUTOPOWER (automatic control of throttles), the elevator is freed to respond solely to glide path navigation requirements, providing precision touchdowns at an exactly correct, fully compensated speed. Available now for medium and larger executive twins at major installation centers. Price $6,200. Send for descriptive literature and specifications.

*Trademark

SAFE FLIGHT INSTRUMENT CORPORATION

WHITE PLAINS, NEW YORK

"Pioneers in Lift Instrumentation"

The system flew at that speed—unless a change was needed to avoid a stall, in which case the autothrottle system's angle of attack mode overrode the manual selection.

AUTOMATING THE ENTIRE FLIGHT

Safe Flight continued to modify and improve the AutoPower system. While it was initially designed for use only during approaches and landings—when pilots have the highest workload—Safe Flight enhanced AutoPower in response to requests from customers to be capable of controlling every aspect of a flight, from takeoff to touchdown. This gave a pilot the option of flying any aspect of the flight either manually or by using AutoPower to control thrust and speed functions.

Among the aircraft on which the enhanced AutoPower was installed was *Speckled Trout*, the code name for a modified Boeing C-135 (essentially the military's Boeing 707) used by the chief of staff of the U.S. Air Force largely to test emerging technologies. Since the original SCAT/AutoPower installation, the system was upgraded four times, including a transition from analog to digital technology.

OVER TIME, SAFE FLIGHT HAS ENHANCED ITS AUTOPOWER SYSTEM TO BE ABLE TO AUTOMATE ANY ASPECT OF A FLIGHT, FROM TAKEOFF TO TOUCHDOWN, GIVING PILOTS OPTIONS FOR WHICH PORTIONS ON A FLIGHT THEY FLY MANUALLY AND WHICH PORTIONS THEY TURN OVER TO AUTOMATION. BELOW, IN A 1982 PHOTO, SAFE FLIGHT TECHNICIANS PREPARE AUTOPOWER CLUTCH HOUSINGS FOR MACHINING.

The commercial aviation industry began changing drastically in the early 1970s as high oil prices forced manufacturers and airlines to reduce costs to remain competitive. Airline engineering staffs were cut back, development stalled, and manufacturers resisted purchasing new equipment unless buyers demanded it. Sales of AutoPower to the commercial market declined. At about the same time, however, corporate aviation began to take interest in the system for installation on aircraft used by CEOs and other senior executives. For managers of corporate aviation departments, AutoPower became an important investment in safety.

The first company to install AutoPower on its fleet was National Distillers and Chemical Corporation, which had approached Gulfstream—supplier of the company's corporate jets—and requested the system. Fitting it into an already packed GII required great ingenuity. It had to be repackaged and made smaller so it could be squeezed into the available space. The AutoPower computer Safe Flight produces with today's components is less than one-eighth the size of the early production design.

"There were always bad places and worse places," Senior Design Engineer Ray Bloch says. "But there was always a place. Probably the hardest one was Cessna's Citation II. There was no room in the pedestal or in the cockpit area, so we ended up having to put the clutch pack way back in the tail. We worked it and solved it."

The popularity among Gulfstream operators of AutoPower on the GII—and later on the GIII—caused Gulfstream to offer the system as an aftermarket option, one that many customers installed. The system proved its value one night when an aircraft lost all of its airspeed display systems. The pilots had no idea how fast they were going, making for a difficult landing. Fortunately the plane had Safe Flight's AutoPower, and, with angle of attack as the speed reference, the pilots successfully landed their aircraft.

AS JOE INSERRO OF TECHNICAL SUPPORT AND SERVICE EXPLAINS, "SAFE FLIGHT IS A CUSTOM COMPANY. EVERY PLANE IS DIFFERENT, SO THE SAME PRODUCT HAS TO BE MADE TO FIT EACH MODEL." AUTOPOWER SYSTEMS HAD TO BE DESIGNED FOR SMALL SPACES, SUCH AS ON THE HAWKER BEECHCRAFT 400, OPPOSITE, AS WELL AS LARGER AIRCRAFT LIKE THE USAF/BOEING RC-135, ABOVE.

3: Growing the Product Line

"When we are considering a supplier, we don't even look at the size of the company. We look at the quality of the product, customer service, and support, as well as the corporate culture."

—Jack Pelton, Chairman, President, and CEO, Cessna Aircraft

By the early 1960s Safe Flight had firmly established itself in the avionics industry and had once again outgrown its facilities. Leonard Greene purchased an old restaurant, The Caroline Lodge, on New King Street adjoining Westchester County Airport, and built a 22,600-square-foot plant on the property. To employees' relief, it was temperature- and humidity-controlled.

The new building easily accommodated Safe Flight's staff of about 50 people, but by the end of the decade the company had to almost double in size to keep pace with the growing workforce needed to meet the demand for Safe Flight's products.

WHEN MAKING KEY DECISIONS IN PRODUCT DEVELOPMENT, LEONARD GREENE USED TO ASK HIMSELF AND HIS STAFF, "IF YOUR LIFE DEPENDED ON GETTING IT DONE, WHAT WOULD YOU DO?" AS THIS AD FOR SAFE FLIGHT'S SCAT AND WIND SHEAR SYSTEMS ON UNITED AIRLINES PLANES POINTS OUT, SAFE FLIGHT BUILT ITS REPUTATION BY CREATING PRODUCTS THAT MAKE AVIATION SAFER.

"The little pipsqueak company," as Leonard had once called Safe Flight, became a major success, and in 1967 it went public. The initial stock offering was priced at $20 per share, and many employees profited when, within months, it rocketed to a high of $66. Seeing an opportunity to accelerate the company's growth, the board of directors eyed the valuable stock as leverage to acquire other companies. The plan was to turn Safe Flight into a major corporation. That was never Leonard's vision, however, and it made him uncomfortable.

"[The board] came to me for approval to buy a specific company," Leonard remembers. "When I looked at this deal, I wondered, why would I want to give up my stock to buy a company I don't like as much as my own? It didn't make sense to me. The board showed me all the numbers and told me that, if I agreed to the acquisition, I could retire to an island off the coast of France. I thought about that. Then I explained to them that retiring was not my business objective. Safe Flight had too many parts of me in it. I enjoyed running the nuts and bolts of the business, and the value of it to me could not be found on a ledger page. Getting bigger to get bigger was of no interest to me. The board and I then decided that my goals were not the same as theirs. And so I bought back our stock, and we returned to being a private company."

Leonard's decision to buy back Safe Flight's stock ensured that the company would remain small in an industry that came to be dominated by mammoth corporations. While the disadvantages appear obvious—in critical mass, financial leverage, economy of scale, and market muscle, for example—Leonard believed that remaining small and compact offered unique competitive advantages.

Fewer layers of management, he felt, made it substantially easier for the company to respond to customers' requests, to rapidly turn ideas into products, and to make and implement decisions.

WIND SHEAR

Safe Flight's ability to apply its innovative technology to new problems was put to the test in June 1975, after an Eastern Airlines Boeing 727 flight crashed on final approach to New York's John F. Kennedy Airport. More than 100 people died.

Using data recovered from the cockpit and flight data recorders, investigators discovered that the accident had been caused by a wind shear—a hazard newly recognized

STAYING SMALL FOR A REASON

Safe Flight managers point to many advantages of Safe Flight's being a small company—for instance, in 2007, when Bombardier wanted to replace a competitor's AoA vane on its CL-605 business jet. Tom Grunbeck, Safe Flight's vice president for sales and marketing, says, "We were able to produce a prototype before our competition was able to submit a proposal.

"Generally we can produce a product from order through certification in less than a year," Grunbeck says. "Because Safe Flight's engineers work with our clients through the entire certification process, which most companies don't do, we can save manufacturers a substantial amount of time. We put our people in their test airplanes to change the parameters of our equipment during the flight. With flight testing costing as much as $25,000 an hour, that can add up to a substantial savings."

Safe Flight also proved its quick-to-market capabilities when it rapidly created a completely new product following a discussion with Embraer about angle of attack sensors. "They told us they needed to monitor the heaters on the external sensors," says Robert Teter, vice president of research and development, explaining that the probes are heated to prevent ice from forming on the tubes; if the heater fails in icing conditions and the pilot doesn't know it, the loss of air data can be critical. "Within three months we'd designed a heater current monitor for the Embraer Phenom 100, and in another three months we had a prototype being tested," Teter says.

For Safe Flight customers like Embraer, Bombardier, and others, the size of the company matters less than its ability to deliver—consistently. "When we are considering a supplier, we don't even look at the size of the company," says Cessna's Chairman, President, and CEO Jack Pelton. "We look at the quality of the product, customer service, and support, as well as the corporate culture, because when you put something on the airplane, you want to make certain you're going to have support for the life cycle of that plane. Safe Flight certainly is a small company based on its financial size, but in the eyes of Cessna—considering the types of products they offer—they really are a giant in the industry."

Furthermore, the continuity of Safe Flight's workforce—which Leonard attributed largely to the company's size, intimacy, and unique culture—

JOE TISEO, LEFT, AND WINSTON WOO, FRONT ROW; AND BOB TETER, JOE GORDON, AND TOM SCOFIELD, LEFT TO RIGHT, BACK ROW, RUN DIAGNOSTIC SOFTWARE ON A NEW SAFE FLIGHT STALL WARNING PROGRAM.

ensured that Safe Flight could hold onto its institutional knowledge and could design and manufacture products with high quality—while forging strong, lasting relationships with customers.

Workers, who often move among jobs at Safe Flight depending on their desires and the company's needs, second such an opinion. "We're pretty lean, so most of us do many different things," says Senior Project Engineer Paul Levine. "I don't just sit down and write specifications as I probably would at a larger company. I also get to design and build circuits. I discuss with production how we're going to build things. I talk directly to our customers. I talk to quality control. I usually have a list of 20 to 30 things I need to get done. And because so many of us have been here so long, almost always when I go into the back or pick up the phone, I'm working with someone I've known for years and worked with many times before. That's a big plus."

There's an ascending career path at Safe Flight for people who want it, as John Banks' experience—rather typical for longtime Safe Flight employees, shows: "My first job was as an hourly employee on the electrical assembly line," he says. "I'm now the facility manager." Greg Tassio started at Safe Flight as an assembler in 1979 and then moved into technical repair. He eventually became the supervisor of the mechanical assembly department and is now Safe Flight's production manager.

THE FAA ESTIMATES THAT
BETWEEN 1964 AND 1985
WIND SHEAR WAS A CON-
TRIBUTING FACTOR IN 26
MAJOR AVIATION ACCIDENTS,
CAUSING 620 DEATHS AND 200
INJURIES. SINCE 1995 ON-
BOARD WIND SHEAR DETECTION
SYSTEMS—PIONEERED BY SAFE
FLIGHT—HAVE COMBINED WITH
GROUND RADAR TO REDUCE
THAT TO APPROXIMATELY ONE
ACCIDENT EVERY DECADE. THE
GRAPHIC OPPOSITE ILLUSTRATES
THE HAZARD OF WIND SHEAR
OR MICROBURST WINDS.

to be a downburst or microburst of wind that occurs in a thunderstorm. Wind shear has come to be defined as any rapid change in wind speed and/or direction—horizontal or vertical. Research revealed that wind shears near ground level had been a primary factor in at least 25 accidents before the 1975 JFK crash, many of them involving fatalities. Most had initially been attributed to pilot error.

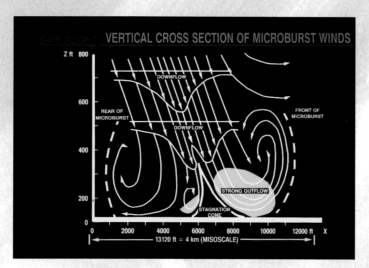

VERTICAL CROSS SECTION OF MICROBURST WINDS

Z ft 800

600

400

200

0

DOWNFLOW

DOWNFLOW

REAR OF MICROBURST

FRONT OF MICROBURST

STRONG OUTFLOW

STAGNATION CONE

0   2000   4000   6000   8000   10000   12000 ft   X

13120 ft = 4 km (MISOSCALE)

Because there was no way to predict a wind shear encounter, it was all but impossible for pilots to respond to one. Leonard felt that pilots were unfairly taking the blame for wind shear accidents and that the industry needed to give them a tool to help them cope with this rare condition. As he said in a speech to an aviation industry audience when he was honored with The Flight Safety Foundation Meritorious Award in 1981, "It is time to stop saying there must be something wrong with pilots. No longer should the pilot automatically be blamed for landing accidents—now that we recognize, if a downburst is encountered during landing approach, the crew should be properly warned against attempting to land the aircraft."

Wind shear is usually associated with the approach of a storm cell. Initially, it may cause a plane to gain airspeed. In response, most pilots would take the standard action: reduce power to slow the plane down. Under any other circumstance, that's the proper thing to do, but reducing speed can be a perilous response to wind shear. The problem is that wind shear comes with a second phase—a severe headwind component loss and/or downdraft—and that makes it extremely difficult for the airplane to recover if it is already close to the ground. The problem is made worse if the pilot has reduced thrust to correct for the airspeed gain, and the plane can be literally pushed into the ground.

The correct response to a potentially deadly wind shear is to abort the landing as early as possible. But there was no way for pilots to know with certainty that they had encountered a wind shear. Available flight instruments were not capable of measuring wind shear or displaying its impact on a plane's performance—and even if an astute pilot recognized that the aircraft was encountering a wind shear and was not simply caught in a gust, it was often too late to save the airplane. It was clear that devising a reliable early wind shear warning would be the key to saving lives under a condition that at the time was considered a significant hazard to commercial aviation.

ASSOCIATION (NBAA) TRADE SHOW

IS ONE OF A NUMBER OF VENUES

WHERE SAFE FLIGHT HAS SHOWN

ITS NEW PRODUCTS AND MAINTAINS

CLOSE RELATIONSHIPS WITH ITS CUS-

TOMERS. BELOW IS SAFE FLIGHT'S

BOOTH AT THE 1980 SHOW.

ALREADY WORKING ON THE PROBLEM

Within days of the accident at JFK, Ray Bloch approached Leonard Greene. As it turned out, Safe Flight had been working to solve a related problem for several years. Soon after the AutoPower system had been installed on the Douglas DC-9, reports came back from the field that the autothrottles were apparently "hunting" in what was thought to be atmospheric turbulence. When the plane encountered turbulence, the throttles would respond to sudden and usually brief increases in headwind component by increasing— not decreasing—thrust and thus gaining airspeed. AutoPower was trying to counter the horizontal shear. It was trying to anticipate the loss of the wind and discriminating airspeed (as opposed to ground speed) acceleration—a key to smooth autothrottles.

In the Eastern Air Lines accident, the presumption was that the pilot had responded to the sudden increase in airspeed by reducing thrust. That was the proper response— to control indicated airspeed—but when the wind gust passed, the plane was caught in an under-speed condition. Ray Bloch believed it would be possible to build a system to detect a horizontal wind shear simply by employing this feature of the AutoPower system.

Randall, Leonard's son, who had joined Safe Flight as a test pilot and sales engineer a couple of years before the company began working on the wind shear problem, explains, "The next step was my father's recognition that in a thunderstorm-related wind shear, which is by far the most lethal, there is also a vertical component to the wind. We coined the phrase 'downdraft drift angle' to describe that hazard. When we modeled the

Eastern accident, we discovered that, if you were in that condition and recognized it early enough to apply full power and make an avoidance maneuver, it would be possible to escape safely."

Data obtained from simulator trials and in flight tests on both Safe Flight's and customers' aircraft allowed Safe Flight's engineers to compute the mathematical formula needed to create an effective warning system—one that would uniquely calculate the effects of both horizontal and vertical components of a wind shear. Randall says, "It took us more than a year to identify the threshold—the very specific point at which flight crews would have sufficient time to take recovery action—without the unacceptable risk of nuisance warnings from normal turbulence, to develop the other components of the system and to begin testing it."

The actual warning, triggered when sensors detected inertial and air data components of a wind shear, took the form of a voice repeating the words "wind shear" over the cockpit audio system, accompanied by a lighted annunciation.

By late 1976 United Airlines was testing an early Safe Flight wind shear warning system on a Boeing 747 flight training simulator and recording data on a Safe Flight-equipped Boeing 727 in revenue service. Both systems used existing aircraft sensors to measure air mass parameters.

Boeing's study of data from the 1975 Eastern crash indicated that the pilots could have saved their plane by applying power, changing the pitch angle and aborting the landing about five seconds earlier than they had—if they had been warned. Under conditions that simulated the accident, the Safe Flight system provided a warning alert with nine seconds' lead. In the simulator, when flight crews confronted a wind shear without any warning, almost all of the planes crashed. But in every instance in which the crew received a warning that provided the few additional seconds, all of the evaluation flight crews were able to maneuver safely through the wind shear using normal piloting technique.

The industry's first wind shear warning device, called the Safe Flight Wind Shear Warning System, received its initial FAA Supplemental Type certification in 1979 on a Learjet 36A. Introducing this vital safety product, Randall wrote in a press release that the company expected the system to have "as significant an impact on the safety of flight as the development of the pre-stall warning had in the 1940s."

RANDALL GREENE, SAFE FLIGHT'S PRESIDENT AND CEO, FIRST FLEW A PLANE WHEN HE WAS NINE YEARS OLD. "I'VE ALWAYS HAD A PASSION TO FLY AIRPLANES," HE SAYS. IN HIS CAREER AS A TEST PILOT AND AVIONICS COMPANY EXECUTIVE, HE HAS FLOWN NEARLY EVERYTHING FROM GLIDERS TO THE GOODYEAR BLIMP. IN 1974 HE WAS TEST PILOT IN PRINCETON UNIVERSITY'S AIRBORNE FLIGHT DEVELOPMENT RYAN NAVION, ABOVE.

LEONARD GREENE'S LEGACY

For its first 50 years most of Safe Flight's innovation came from the mind of Leonard Greene. Greene turned Safe Flight's pilot seat over to his son Randall in 2001, following the death of his son Donald and a diagnosis of terminal lung cancer. After a courageous five-year battle, Leonard died at the age of 88 on November 30, 2006, leaving an extraordinary legacy.

For almost seven decades Leonard was one of America's most productive and successful inventors. His name is on more than 100 patents—for inventions including the stall warning system, a system that prevents heat-seeking missiles from shooting down helicopters, eyeglasses that correct color-blindness, a bullet that can penetrate wood without leaving a hole, and a supersonic passenger plane capable of flying 50 percent faster than the Concorde while using less fuel per passenger than a Boeing 747. In 1991 he entered the National Inventors Hall of Fame—inducted by his friend, former Mercury astronaut and U.S. Senator, John Glenn.

Leonard received numerous other awards, including Flight Safety Foundation's Air Safety Award in 1949 and 1981 and, in 1999, the Bendix Trophy for Aviation Safety—the latter a prestigious award given to him, as the citation reads, for "invention and implementation of revolutionary safety devices during his career of more than 50 years as an aerodynamicist, engineering test pilot, specialist in aircraft performance and control, and theoretician in supersonic flight." He also received the 1996 National Business Aircraft Award for Meritorious Service, wrote two books on public policy, was elected an associate fellow of the American Institute of Aeronautics, and was a very proud Life Member of the Society of Experimental Test Pilots. Other awards included the Albert Gallatin Award for Civic Leadership among Businessmen in the Northeastern States and a Private Sector Initiative Commendation from the President of the United States. He also founded a think tank on economic policy and co-founded the Corporate Angel Network, which

IN HIS BOOK *INVENTORSHIP*, LEONARD GREENE WROTE, "SUCCESS WILL DEPEND ON THE SIZE OF YOUR THINKING, ALONG WITH THE EFFORT YOU INVEST IN IT." HE IS SEEN BELOW WITH JOHN GLENN AT HIS INDUCTION INTO THE NATIONAL INVENTORS HALL OF FAME.

provides free air transportation for cancer patients traveling for treatment, using empty seats on corporate jets.

While Leonard enjoyed the many honors and the awards he received, the patents that covered an entire wall of his office were more a reflection of the life he lived. He went through life exploring ideas and collecting a wide and truly unusual assortment of friends. Among them were Senators Barry Goldwater and John McGovern, who couldn't have been further apart politically. One of Randall's favorite memories of Leonard is of how he loved to fly the series of amphibious aircraft that Safe Flight owned, land on lakes, open the door, and stick out a fishing pole—a practice that often got him into trouble with the Army Corps of Engineers, which didn't like people landing on its lakes without permission.

"Once, I remember, he went on a fishing trip, and minutes after he landed and started fishing, somebody came up—the local police, I think," Randall says. "He was ready for that. He always carried letters in his plane from both Goldwater and McGovern, and the letters were very similar. They explained that Leonard was a great person and a personal friend, and so on. What Leonard would do is talk to the officer for a few minutes, just long enough to get some idea of the officer's political leanings. When he figured out whether the officer was red or blue, he'd pull out the appropriate letter to show him. He usually got to stay around and fish."

Leonard continued working right up to his death on three new patents

and on a book that proposed a redesign of the economic structure of America. Characteristically, even in his later years, his mind remained focused on the future. "I already know about today," he would say. "I'm thinking about tomorrow."

Perhaps Glenn summed up the true value of Leonard Greene's life's work when he said, "If Elmer Sperry [the inventor of the gyroscope and the automatic pilot] showed aircraft pilots the way home, it was Leonard Greene who ensured their safe arrival."

IN THE 1980s SAFE FLIGHT ADVERTISED ITS SPEED COMMAND SYSTEMS AS SOLUTIONS TO A VARIETY OF AVIATION PROBLEMS— AMONG THEM WIND SHEAR. IT WAS THE 1985 CRASH OF A LOCKHEED L-1011, LIKE THE ONE OPPOSITE, THAT SPURRED MANY AVIATION FLEETS TO INSTALL WIND SHEAR WARNING SYSTEMS.

RECOVERY GUIDANCE

Safe Flight's Wind Shear Warning System alerted pilots to a potential for disaster, but pilots still had to take corrective action to save their airplanes. The FAA developed specific guidelines for pilots to follow when they encountered wind shear conditions, but even with a warning they still had only a few seconds to perform the recommended escape maneuver. They had to get it right the first time.

To help pilots make the right decision, Safe Flight created the Recovery Guidance System, an enhancement to Safe Flight's SCAT that instantly calculates the proper pitch angle for a safe escape. When a wind shear alarm sounds, a pilot has to pay attention to only one instrument: the recovery guidance pitch attitude command on SCAT. He simply applies maximum thrust and follows the pitch command bars on the flight director, and the system automatically executes the best possible climb profile. As Leonard Greene said, "We show pilots the route to safety."

Not long after certification of its Wind Shear Warning System in 1979, Safe Flight installed hundreds of systems in more than 40 different types of corporate, commercial, and military aircraft. Because of differences between planes, each installation meant a new technical challenge. Safe Flight's engineers solved these after considerable investments in time, effort, and ingenuity.

As quick as the industry in general was to adopt Safe Flight's Wind Shear Warning System, it was some time before the major airlines were convinced. Two events, within two years of each other, sold them.

On a sunny afternoon in August 1983, *Air Force One*, carrying President Ronald Reagan, landed at Washington's Andrews Air Force base. It was an ordinary landing— but five minutes after the plane touched down, a potentially deadly wind shear swept across the airfield, sparing the president's plane but causing extensive damage throughout the airport. It was a close call that could have changed history, and it served as a strong reminder that the wind shear problem had not been fully solved. Two years later, in August 1985, a Delta Airlines Lockheed L-1011 crashed at Dallas-Fort Worth International Airport; 137 people died, and wind shear was determined to have been the cause. Within months Safe Flight's wind shear system was being installed on new production and retrofitted on older airline and corporate aviation fleets.

Safe Flight has continued to develop the Wind Shear Warning System for a variety

of aircraft and applications, and it is currently available in both analog and digital config-
urations. The company is also producing an integrated package that combines the wind
shear warning and SCAT systems for the business jet market.

"This is something we've wanted to do for a long time," Randall Greene says.
"Because of its size and cost, this was the type of product that once would have been
limited to the largest transport aircraft. We're only able to do it now because the hardware technology has gotten to the point where it's small enough, light enough, and
inexpensive enough to be successful even for the smallest corporate jets."

SINCE THE DEADLY CRASH OF A
DELTA AIRLINER IN 1985 AT
DALLAS-FORT WORTH INTERNA-
TIONAL AIRPORT, OPPOSITE, SAFE
FLIGHT'S PIONEERING WORK HAS
HELPED SUBSTANTIALLY REDUCE
THE NUMBER OF ACCIDENTS
CAUSED BY WIND SHEAR—
ALLOWING PILOTS TO COUNTER
OR AVOID THE DANGERS OF THIS
POWERFUL AND HIGHLY LOCAL-
IZED WEATHER PHENOMENON.
SAFE FLIGHT ALSO HAS MADE
FLYING SAFER FOR PILOTS OF
INNOVATIVE MILITARY AIRCRAFT,
SUCH AS THE A-10 THUNDERBOLT,
RIGHT. THE COMPANY USED ITS
EXPERTISE IN LIFT DETECTION
AND STALL WARNING TECHNOL-
OGY TO CONTROL THE ANGLE OF
ATTACK AND PREVENT ENGINE
FLAME-OUTS IN HIGH-LIFT,
HIGH-G MANEUVERS.

BACK TO THE FUTURE

What has allowed Safe Flight's products to endure—the original stall warning detector is now more than 60 years old, autothrottles were developed 40 years ago, and wind shear detection was introduced more than 25 years ago—is the ability of the company to keep pace with emerging technologies, to update proven tools for new aircraft and integration applications, and to work closely with customers to innovatively solve unique problems.

In 1976 the United States Air Force introduced the A-10 Thunderbolt (better known as the *Warthog*). Built by Fairchild-Republic, the A-10 was designed to provide close air support for ground troops by destroying tanks and other armored vehicles. To accomplish that mission, the plane had to be capable of rapid dives and climbs, as well as tight turns close to the ground.

Fairchild-Republic had mounted the aircraft's twin engines high on the rear of the fuselage, in part to shield them from ground attacks. It was an unusual design, and at high angles of attack—for example, during a steep turn or climb—the airflow off the wings could block the engine air intakes, causing a compressor stall or flame-out. The A-10 program office approached Safe Flight to work on a system to protect against it. In addition to protecting the A-10 against a wing stall, Safe Flight's solution drew upon the company's understanding of the high angle of attack capabilities of its wing lift and stall warning technology to give the A-10 system other required modes. Safe Flight developed its stall warning computer to activate leading edge lift devices at high angles of attack, protecting the airflow into the engines at high angles of attack and G-loads. The A-10 could then operate at a substantially higher angle of attack than would have been safely possible otherwise —and with this essential modification, the A-10 went into full production.

Safe Flight went on to develop several other systems for the A-10, which ended up performing magnificently throughout a storied history. At one point it was slated to be phased out, but it proved its ability in the 1991 Gulf War and, more recently, in Afghanistan and Iraq. The A-10 is now scheduled to stay in service in the Air Force until 2028.

THE N₁ COMPUTER

In his time with Safe Flight, Randall Greene has been no stranger to product development, having played an important role in one of Safe Flight's key products of the 1990s, the N₁ Computer. That product came into existence while he was obtaining an FAA Type rating to fly the Hawker Beechcraft 400—a small, twin-engine corporate jet—so that he could develop, FAA-certify, and demonstrate Safe Flight's AutoPower system to potential customers. After training at FlightSafety's Level-D simulator in Wichita, Kansas, he was licensed to fly the Hawker 400—before he'd ever sat in one.

When he went to Raytheon Aircraft Services' Atlanta facility to install AutoPower in the airplane, he arrived at the field before his copilot and decided to begin his preflight check. Unfortunately, he couldn't get into the aircraft—because there was no equivalent to the cabin door on the simulator, which was the one thing he hadn't been taught to operate at FlightSafety. Eventually, however, he settled into the captain's seat. As he prepared for takeoff, his copilot leaned forward and taped the blank side of a business card to the instrument panel. On the card the pilot had written a long list of numbers.

"What's that?" Randall asked.

THE N$_1$ COMPUTER ACCURATELY
PROVIDES NECESSARY THRUST
SETTINGS FOR FOUR BASIC FLIGHT
MODES. ITS DISPLAY IS SEEN
ABOVE. RIGHT, A PERFORMANCE
MANUAL OF THE TYPE PILOTS
PREVIOUSLY HAD TO CONSULT
IN FLIGHT.

AS SAFE FLIGHT EXPLAINS, THE N₁
COMPUTER "TAKES BY-THE-BOOK
FLIGHT OPERATIONS AND MAKES
THEM BETTER THAN THE BOOK"—
AND BY DOING SO, ELIMINATES PART
OF THE COCKPIT WORKLOAD.

"It's an N_1 cheat sheet I made up," his copilot explained casually.

The N_1 target changes continually during a flight as the altitude and temperature change. To determine the proper N_1 setting, pilots have to consult the performance charts provided by the aircraft's manufacturer. While consulting charts during flight seemed simple enough, Randall knew from his own experience that that was not the way pilots operate in the real world. When a plane is climbing at, say, 3,000 feet per minute, the pilot doesn't have time to consult a manual to determine the next power setting every minute or so. Instead, most pilots use conservative general engine speed or temperature settings rather than looking up the recommended settings for each flight condition—a compromise that sacrifices performance and fuel.

He was astounded. "We were sitting in a multi-million-dollar airplane," he recalls, "and it was equipped with at least another million dollars worth of avionics—and this pilot wouldn't fly it without a hand-written card taped to the panel."

In early 1995 Randall asked Safe Flight's engineers to design a small computer—small enough to replace the panel-mounted N_1 thumbwheel "reminder"—that would give pilots the desired engine settings. About seven months later, Safe Flight produced a prototype N_1 Computer. Safe Flight FAA-certified the N_1 Computer for several Hawker, Cessna Citation, and Dassault Falcon models.

THE NEXT GENERATION

By the year 2000 Leonard Greene had successfully led Safe Flight through the turbulent ups and downs of the highly competitive, continually evolving aviation industry for more than five decades. The company had literally opened its barn doors a year before the sound barrier was broken and had prospered well into the era of supersonic flight.

As Leonard reached his 80s, he began to look to his family to lead the company. Two of his sons, Donald and Randall, had long shared his passion for flight. Like so many children of Safe Flight employees, they had practically grown up inside the company, working there during summers and attending company events. Randall jokes, "Depending on how much trouble we were in at home, we worked in various areas. One summer, for example, Don painted lines in the parking lot."

Eventually both brothers went to work for Safe Flight full-time. In 1980 Randall left the company and went to work for the Bendix General Aviation Avionics Division. In 1988 he founded the Commander Aircraft Company, purchasing the single-engine Rockwell 112/114 product line from Gulfstream and beginning manufacture of the 114B Commander. After taking Commander public in 1991, he sold his interest and settled happily in Colorado with his family—taking on roles with Safe Flight in the development, testing, and sale of new products.

Don Greene was Leonard's natural successor. Don had worked at Safe Flight since the mid-1980s. Although being the boss' kid can be difficult, Don had a natural warmth and a work ethic that made him popular with other employees. After Ralph Friedman retired in 1988, Don was named executive vice president and began shouldering more of his father's responsibilities.

DONALD GREENE HELD MANY JOBS AT SAFE FLIGHT, STARTING WITH PAINTING LINES IN THE PARKING LOT AND ENDING WITH HIS NEAR-APPOINTMENT AS PRESIDENT. THE PLAN WAS CUT SHORT IN 2001, HOWEVER, WHEN HE WAS KILLED ABOARD UNITED FLIGHT 93 ON 9/11. A BROWN UNIVERSITY CLASSMATE RECALLED, "THOSE OF US WHO WERE LUCKY ENOUGH TO KNOW HIM WERE BETTER FOR IT."

With a five-year age difference between Randall and Don, the two brothers hadn't been particularly close growing up, but once they started working together at Safe Flight they forged a strong relationship. As Randall recalls, "We flew together, sailed together, and we worked hard together. It was still very much our father's company, but we certainly were contributing. We complemented each other perfectly. Don loved the details of business, and he loved going through every inch of the factory, working with contractors and suppliers. But he didn't like to travel. He much preferred spending every minute possible with his family. I loved developing and demonstrating our products, so I did many of the other things that had to be done. Don graciously called it a partnership, but it wasn't. It was going to be his business."

The two brothers usually spoke by telephone several times a day, and every month

THE "CHALLENGE"
FROM BOMBARDIER

At the 1998 National Business Aircraft Association convention in Dallas, Karl Genest, director of product planning for Bombardier's popular Challenger 604, a wide-body corporate aircraft, walked into the Safe Flight booth and posed a question. His company had decided to offer an autothrottle system as an option. A Safe Flight competitor had estimated that it would take three years and several million dollars of non-recurring charges to put autothrottles into the airplane. He wondered if Safe Flight could do better.

RESPONDING TO A CHALLENGE FROM BOMBARDIER, SAFE FLIGHT DEVELOPED AN AUTOTHROTTLE SYSTEM FOR THE COMPANY'S CHALLENGER 604—DESIGNING IT, CONSTRUCTING IT, AND GETTING IT FAA-CERTIFIED IN LESS THAN A YEAR.

Safe Flight had worked previously with Bombardier to install angle of attack instrumentation on a large number of Challenger 600 and 601s. It took Safe Flight slightly less than a year to get its autothrottle system designed, developed, and FAA-certified on the Challenger 604. Bombardier unveiled the option at the 1999 NBAA show.

In 2001 Safe Flight enhanced AutoPower for the 604, adding a second servo motor so that the system would drive each throttle separately. This dual-servo system allowed engineers to include an N_1 sync control. N_1 refers to the engine turbine speed, which the pilot controls through the thrust levers to set engine power. "Enhanced" AutoPower became the most popular option on the Challenger 604; it has since become standard equipment on the new Challenger 605. Autothrottles have also been certified on Bombardier's CRJ 200 and is a popular production option on the Challenger 850 series.

For more than four decades, AutoPower has been an important product for Safe Flight—having been installed on more than 9,000 airplanes since its introduction. Once available only on airliners and large business jets, the enhanced system has been adapted for mid-size business jets, a rapidly growing market. It has also been reengineered to function smoothly in all-electronic FADEC (Full Authority Digital Electronics Control) engine control systems, in which a dedicated computer and related accessories control all aspects of an aircraft's performance. Working with Gulfstream, Safe Flight has developed a FADEC AutoPower system for the Gulfstream G200 and is currently developing AutoPower for Gulfstream's latest mid-sized business jet, the G150.

Randall spent a few days in Westchester. "We'd work all day, going over new products and sales programs, a whole host of things. Then we'd go have dinner and bourbon. It was in so many ways an idyllic time."

PASSING THE TORCH

In mid-2001 Leonard Greene announced that Don would become president of Safe Flight, effective in early 2002. It was set to be a smooth transition—but it never took place.

On the morning of September 11, 2001, Don boarded United Flight 93 in Newark, New Jersey, planning to join his other brothers in California for a hiking trip. What happened next has become the darkest day in American history: soon after takeoff, terrorists hijacked the Boeing 757; passengers tried to wrest control of the aircraft from the hijackers, and the plane later crashed in a Pennsylvania field. Ironically, had passengers gained control of the airplane, Don could have flown it.

"We were just devastated," says Mary Blancato, Leonard Greene's secretary for more than four decades. "So many of us had known Donnie for so long. We'd watched him grow up. For so many of us, it truly was a death in our family."

The day Don Greene died, Randall told his wife, Anne, "We're going to be moving." That was not what he wanted to do. He and his family enjoyed their Colorado lifestyle, but he faced reality. He wasn't simply the *logical* choice to lead Safe Flight; after his brother's death, he was the *only* choice.

When Randall was growing up, his father had advised him, "Don't be a pilot. Be a doctor or a businessman, and buy an airplane. Then hire a pilot to fly you around." He paid little attention. He was about nine years old when he flew an airplane for the first time; it was his father's Beechcraft Model 18, and he had to sit on a pile of chart books to see out the windshield. Both sons soloed for the first time on Friday, August 13, 1964, a date neither one of them ever forgot. Don was at a flying camp in Connecticut, and his solo flight was the culmination of the program—but when Randall heard that his younger brother was going to solo that day, he decided, "No way Donnie's going to solo before I do." Early that morning, he went to Westchester County Airport and pleaded with a reluctant instructor to let him solo. No one knows which brother was alone in the air first that day.

After leaving graduate school in 1971, Randall flew fire patrol for the U.S. Forest Service in New Mexico in the summer and worked as a charter pilot for Taos Ski Valley in the winter. Joining Safe Flight in 1973, he rolled up his sleeves and soon was helping develop the Wind Shear Warning System, among other programs. He has learned to fly nearly every kind of aircraft, from jets to single-engine planes to gliders to helicopters—even the Goodyear blimp.

Days after his brother's death, Randall returned to Westchester. He offered his devastated father help in any capacity Leonard wanted and soon found himself spending considerable time in the office. Several months later, Leonard asked him, "Are you ready to move?"

Randall nodded.

"You can run the business," Leonard said.

The period following Don Greene's death was the beginning of what was perhaps the most challenging time in Safe Flight's history.

In 1990 the company had contracted to integrate most of its products—angle of attack, SCAT, AutoPower, wind shear warning, and its RAT/EPR computers—into the avionics system of the Air Force's RC-135. It was an extraordinarily complicated program, an enormous amount of work was required, and the penalties for failure to meet contractual deadlines could have bankrupted the company.

Then, the almost unbelievable happened: a month after Don's death, Leonard Greene was diagnosed with advanced lung cancer. Doctors told him he had only months to live.

"I was very lucky that I'd known so many of the people working here for so long," Randall Greene remembers. "It was a rough time for everybody, and there were many sleepless nights. But I had tremendous support from the entire company. This was the time that the Safe Flight culture my father had established and nurtured truly paid off. Everyone worked together to get us through this period."

The integrated RC-135 suite of Safe Flight systems was delivered, and the customer was satisfied.

4: Gaining Altitude

"Nobody questioned Safe Flight's ability to produce ... and their products still work today on aircraft all over the world."

—Tony Hall, Senior Project Engineer for Tactical Surveillance Systems Platforms,

L3 Communications Integrated Systems

F ulfilling Safe Flight's contract with the Air Force required an extraordinary effort. "It probably wasn't a realistic schedule," acknowledges Tony Hall of L3 Communications Integrated Systems, the company that worked with Safe Flight on the project. "What we wanted to do was take five separate functions and combine them into one box. It's a very complex piece of equipment. When we asked Safe Flight if they could build an aircraft performance computer from scratch, they agreed to take it on."

SUCCESSFULLY FULFILLING A CONTRACT TO BUILD A COMPLEX PERFORMANCE COMPUTER FOR THE AIR FORCE RC-135 ON A NEARLY IMPOSSIBLE SCHEDULE REQUIRED THE EXPERTISE, TEAM- WORK, AND TOTAL DEDICATION OF THE ENTIRE SAFE FLIGHT STAFF— AMONG THEM, OPPOSITE, VAL D'OTTAVIO, SENIOR MECHANICAL DRAFTSMAN; EDWARD SURPRIS AND ROBERT CACHAY, CAD OPERATORS; AND JANE WONG, DESIGN CHECKER, SEEN HERE EXAMINING A THROTTLE QUAD- RANT PROTOTYPE FOR A NEW SINGLE-ENGINE VERY LIGHT JET (VLJ).

Hall, L3's senior product engineer for Tactical Surveillance Systems Platforms, said one of Safe Flight's assets was its flexibility. "Lots of times when you're working with a larger corporation, there is some real inflexibility. Safe Flight was more amenable to trying things to satisfy the customer, as opposed to sticking to the initial requirements. When you're developing things over several years, technology changes, processes change, capabilities are added, and they were always willing to try the next best thing. They also supported us tremendously during testing. They had people down in Greenville, Texas, 24 hours a day. I remember being in the lab with their guys at two and three o'clock in the morning, trying to work out issues after test flights. We were able to put the system on the RC-135 in November of 2002 and certify it early in 2003."

Hall remembers that when the project started, Safe Flight "was lagging in the digital world. I was a bit surprised when I walked in and saw people still working at oak drafting tables that probably dated back to the 1950s, with slide rules, because the components they had supplied previously had been so good. They were the Cadillacs—so nobody questioned their ability to produce what needed to be done. And those products still work today on aircraft all over the world."

Not only did Safe Flight fulfill its contract with the Air Force, Leonard won his initial battle against cancer and lived beyond his doctor's prognosis. "My father liked to joke after he'd successfully landed the airplane, 'Well, we fooled them again,'" Randall says fondly. "Well, he fooled his doctors and his cancer for another five years."

THE FIRST MANAGEMENT TRANSITION

Almost immediately after returning to White Plains, Randall began guiding Safe Flight through the first true management transition in its history. "Safe Flight was a success long before I walked in the door," he says. "We're one of the oldest continuously operating companies in the aerospace industry, and there's a reason for that. I tried to determine what business model made that true, and then I worked on what needed to be done to make certain we could continue to compete successfully in a rapidly changing environment."

Randall quickly instituted changes inside the company—adding new technology and leading a new approach to management—but he didn't tinker with Safe Flight's core values, policies, or culture. He upgraded the computer and communication systems,

SINCE BECOMING PRESIDENT AND CEO OF SAFE FLIGHT IN 2001, RANDALL GREENE HAS LED THE COMPANY THROUGH A COMPLETE MODERNIZATION WHILE MAINTAINING THE CORPORATE VALUES THAT HAVE ALLOWED IT TO FLOURISH IN A HIGHLY COMPETITIVE INDUSTRY FOR MORE THAN SIX DECADES.

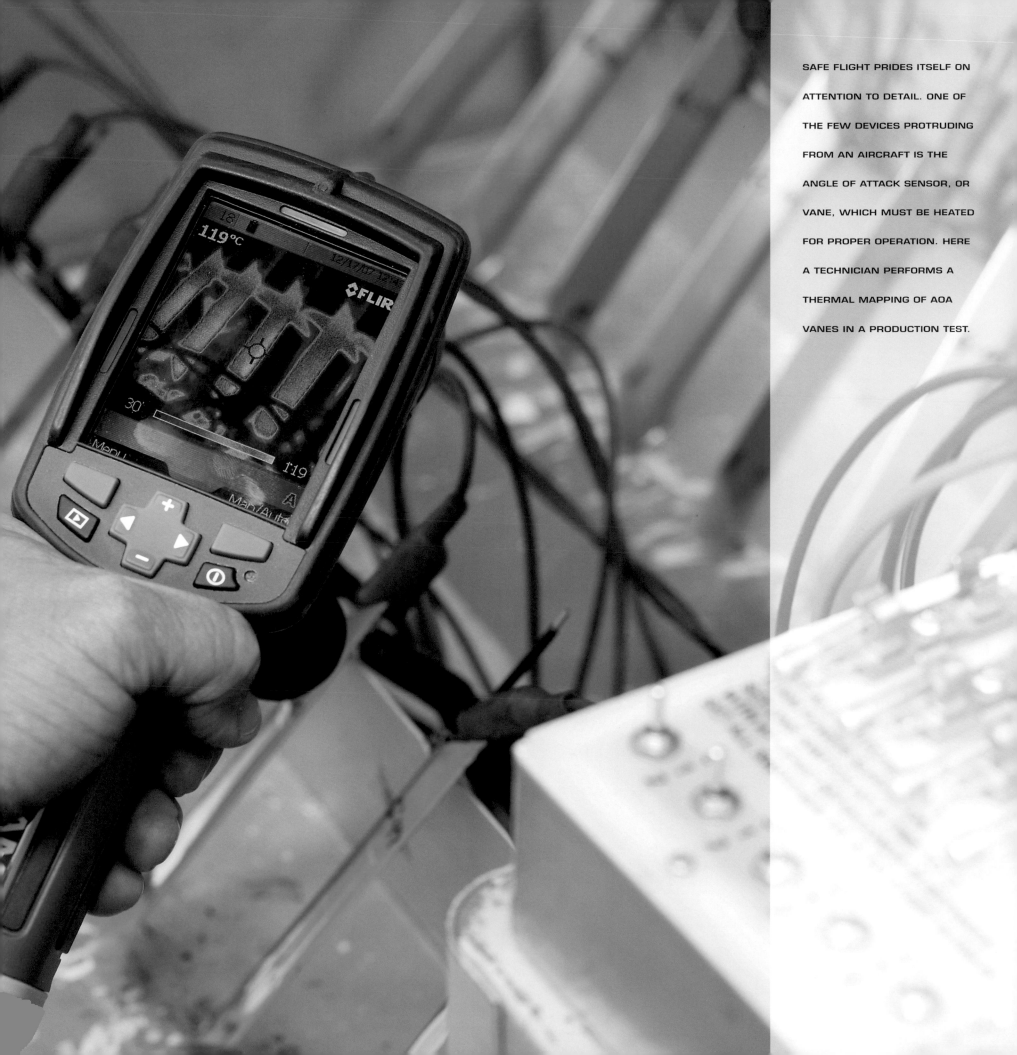

SAFE FLIGHT PRIDES ITSELF ON ATTENTION TO DETAIL. ONE OF THE FEW DEVICES PROTRUDING FROM AN AIRCRAFT IS THE ANGLE OF ATTACK SENSOR, OR VANE, WHICH MUST BE HEATED FOR PROPER OPERATION. HERE A TECHNICIAN PERFORMS A THERMAL MAPPING OF AOA VANES IN A PRODUCTION TEST.

AN AWARDING EXPERIENCE

Safe Flight has been the recipient of numerous awards for the ingenuity and quality of its products.

Among the highlights, the U.S. Department of Defense bestowed an unprecedented honor on Safe Flight when it gave the company its coveted Award for Quality Excellence in two consecutive years, 1982 and 1983. The Small Business Administration also honored the company, naming it the Regional Prime Contractor of the Year in 1982; Leonard Greene was so proud of that particular award that he flew a planeload of Safe Flight employees to Washington, D.C., to accept it with him.

Safe Flight's hiring practices have earned the company a commendation from the secretary of the U.S. Department of Health, Education, and Welfare and a citation from the New York State Governor's Committee to Employ the Handicapped.

Most recently, in the prestigious *Aviation International News* 2005 Product Support Survey, more than 16,000 flight department managers, chief pilots, line captains, first officers, maintenance chiefs, and mechanics ranked Safe Flight first among more than 30 manufacturers, and second in the entire industry in cost of parts, AOG (aircraft on ground) response, and ease of use in its technical manuals—a noteworthy achievement for a small company competing against the giants of the aviation industry.

AMONG THE AWARDS IN SAFE FLIGHT'S DISPLAY CASE ARE, LEFT, A COIN PRESENTED TO LEONARD GREENE UPON HIS 1991 INDUCTION INTO THE NATIONAL INVENTORS HALL OF FAME AND, RIGHT, AN EAGLE PRESENTED TO SAFE FLIGHT IN 1996 BY THE NATIONAL BUSINESS AIRCRAFT ASSOCIATION FOR MERITORIOUS SERVICE TO AVIATION.

THE MELMOTH WAS ORIGINALLY
A TWO-SEAT, HOME-BUILT AIR-
CRAFT CONSTRUCTED BETWEEN
1968 AND 1973 BY PETER
GARRISON, ABOVE. DESIGNED TO
FLY LONG DISTANCES, IT MADE ITS
LONGEST NONSTOP FLIGHT—
2,750 MILES BETWEEN ALASKA
AND JAPAN—IN 1976. GARRISON
BUILT A FOUR-SEAT SUCCESSOR,
THE MELMOTH 2, RIGHT, ANOTHER
LONG-DISTANCE CRAFT. ITS SAFE
FLIGHT SPEED CONTROL SYSTEM,
WHICH WAS TRANSFERRED FROM
THE FIRST MELMOTH, HAS NOW
BEEN FLYING RELIABLY FOR MORE
THAN 35 YEARS.

enabling Safe Flight to revamp its entire operations, from purchasing through delivery; inventory dropped by half while the business grew substantially. For the position of executive vice president, he hired Joe Wilson, a former U.S. Army helicopter pilot in Vietnam who also had an electrical engineering degree from Georgia Tech, a Harvard MBA, and considerable experience in the avionics industry. With Wilson's guidance, Safe Flight modernized all aspects of the facility. They added electronic component manufacturing tools, surface-mount technology, and an array of computer-aided engineering and design tools to improve precision and expand capabilities in design and manufacturing. Those old oak drafting tables and slide rules disappeared as Safe Flight completed the transition to the digital product development world. An old boiler room became a classroom, and Safe Flight began offering technical courses to help employees upgrade their knowledge and skills. They gave the building's exterior a facelift: new sidewalks, fresh landscaping, trees, and parking lot.

When it came to management, Randall says, "Whatever changes I made had to reflect the reality that the management talent at the top would be different from what it had been, with my father and my brother no longer at Safe Flight." Randall set out to develop an effective blend of his father's and his own management styles. A vital change, he knew, was to encourage—in fact, demand—more participation, contribution,

THE F-117 NIGHTHAWK WAS DEVELOPED AND BUILT IN SECRET BY LOCKHEED MARTIN'S SKUNK WORKS IN BURBANK, CALIFORNIA. ALTHOUGH IT TOOK ITS FIRST FLIGHT IN 1981, THE F-117 WASN'T ACKNOWLEDGED BY THE MILITARY UNTIL SEVEN YEARS LATER. AROUND 1988, SAFE FLIGHT RECEIVED A PHONE CALL FROM LOCKHEED MARTIN, ASKING COMPANY EXECUTIVES TO JOIN SKUNK WORKS PRESIDENT SHERMAN N. MULLIN AND AN AIR FORCE GENERAL IN A CEREMONY AT WHICH SAFE FLIGHT WOULD RECEIVE AN AWARD FOR THE PERFORMANCE OF ITS AUTOPOWER SYSTEM ON THE F-117. CONFUSED, SAFE FLIGHT RESPONDED, "WE'RE NOT ON THE 117," TO WHICH LOCKHEED REPLIED, "WHY DO YOU THINK WE'RE CALLED THE SKUNK WORKS?" SAYS SAFE FLIGHT PRESIDENT AND CEO RANDALL GREENE, "WE WERE ON THE F-117 AND DIDN'T EVEN KNOW IT." LOCKHEED HAD RUN ALL OF ITS PURCHASE ORDERS FOR THE F-117 THROUGH ANOTHER PROGRAM.

Lockheed Martin Aeronautics Company
1011 Lockheed Way Palmdale, CA 93599

LOCKHEED MARTIN

April 22, 2008

SAFE FLIGHT INSTRUMENT CORP.
20 NEW KING STREET
WHITE PLAINS, NY 10604

Dear Randall Greene,CEO

The retirement of the F-117 Program is a time for reflection on the role SAFE FLIGHT INSTRUMENT CORP. has played supporting the Program. Lockheed Martin Aeronautics would like to take this opportunity to acknowledge the contributions of SAFE FLIGHT INSTRUMENT CORP. staff at every level for their commitment to producing a quality product to ensure the safety, dependability and effectiveness of the F-117 aircraft.

SAFE FLIGHT INSTRUMENT CORP. has been an integral and key part of the Team Nighthawk workforce linked to the F-117 Mission Statement:

> *Be an engaged, innovative workforce, supporting the F-117 precision strike aircraft –*
> *Achieving new standards in affordability, reliability and survivability.*

We thank you and honor you as part of the indelible history of the F-117 aircraft, a history whose roots trace back to 1974 when the idea for a stealth fighter was thrust to reality.

Sincerely,

Dr. George F. Zielsdorff
Vice President U-2 & F-117

JOE GORDON, SENIOR VICE PRESI-
DENT OF ENGINEERING, ABOVE,
HAS BEEN AT SAFE FLIGHT SINCE
1963—LONG ENOUGH, HE JOKES,
"FOR MY KIDS TO BE HERE AND
THEIR KIDS TO BE HERE." HIS
TENURE IS NOT QUITE SUFFICIENT
TO HAVE ALLOWED HIM INVOLVE-
MENT IN THE INSTALLATION OF AN
EARLY STALL WARNING INDICATOR
ON THIS CESSNA 195, WHICH SAFE
FLIGHT BUILT BETWEEN 1947 AND
1954. THIS IS THE PERSONAL
AIRCRAFT OF JACK PELTON,
CHAIRMAN, CEO, AND PRESIDENT
OF CESSNA. OPPOSITE, NITIN
PANCHAL, DESIGN ENGINEER,
TESTS THE CIRCUITRY ON AN
AUTOTHROTTLE COMPUTER.

and buy-in from key managers. He wanted the reward, as well as the pressure, of making important decisions to be shared with those managers.

Randall says, "I wanted to create a decision-making environment in which we have a balance of consensus but only one vote. I'm the one who has that vote, but I want department leaders who have responsibility for their parts of the organization and are invested in the process. When we get to the point where a decision is made, I want everybody to be on board with it."

Randall Greene had established and run his own company, he had worked at Safe Flight in different positions for several years, and he was intimately familiar with the company's corporate culture—so, while establishing a new management structure took time and energy, there were established models to follow. What was more of a chal-lenge was replacing his father's creative contributions. Leonard had been the creative force behind most of Safe Flight's products for more than 60 years. Randall and his design team needed to generate more ideas for new products and new markets.

There was no arguing the success of this management approach. By 2007 Safe Flight's revenues had nearly tripled from the day Randall Greene took control.

"LOOKS LIKE I'M GOING TO STAY"

Employees with only three decades of tenure are considered newcomers at Safe Flight. Many people have worked for the company for more than 40 years, with some nearing 50 years of service.

Sam Cambriello was in his 48th year at Safe Flight in 2007. Ed Manacke started in 1956 and, with the exception of a three-year break, has been there ever since. Engineers Joe Gordon and Peter Cordes have been there 44 years. Bill Forrester sort of retired after 44 years, only to continue working part-time. Bill Korr, with 43 years, jokes, "It looks like I'm going to stay." Forty-one-year Safe Flight veteran John Banks adds, "I expect to be here another 40 years." Bill McIntosh celebrated 42 years at the company in 2007, and Mary Blancato was one year behind him, at 41.

"I came here to work in 1983," Carmen Bairasso explains. "So now I can retire, but when I think about it, I say, maybe I'm going to work here for another six months. Then the six months pass, and I say, maybe just six months more. For me, I'm really happy in the morning when I get to come in to work. The people here, these are my friends."

Part of the reason for Safe Flight employees' extraordinary loyalty to the company is that founder Leonard Greene set out to establish a company that would be loyal to its workers. During periods when business slumped, management created ways to keep employees busy rather than let them go. "We'd paint the plant if things got slow," Cambriello recalls. "We'd do extra cleaning; we'd take the lights out of the sockets and wash them. We'd go outside and do some landscaping. It always worked out."

When skyrocketing fuel prices pushed the airline industry into a recession

TRUE TO THE VISION OF ITS FOUNDER, SAFE FLIGHT HAS BECOME A "SECOND FAMILY" TO ITS EMPLOYEES. TODAY'S SAFE FLIGHT EMPLOYEES— SEEN HERE ON THE LAWN IN FRONT OF THE COMPANY'S FACILITY IN WHITE PLAINS, NEW YORK, IN 2007—INCLUDE MANY WHO HAVE BEEN WITH THE COMPANY FOR MORE THAN FOUR DECADES.

in the early 2000s, Safe Flight had to consider drastic action. Management had to choose between two options: either a substantial number of people would have to be laid off, or the entire workforce could voluntarily cut back to a four-day work week, with everybody sharing the financial pain equally—including the officers, who worked five days a week and were paid for only four. The decision for a four-day week was made; the company also arranged for every eligible worker to receive payment from the unemployment office for that lost day. The reduced schedule lasted almost a year, and, while a small number of employees eventually left the company, there were few layoffs.

Employee longevity is an important competitive advantage for a small company like Safe Flight, says Randall Greene, the company's chief executive officer and president. "We've made an investment in continuity," he says. "We know we're only as good as the people who come here to work every day."

Senior Project Engineer Paul Levine explains: "What we have here is a very strong peer-to-peer relationship. Everybody has been here a long time and done it all. We know what the problems are and how to deal with them. Of course, we panic all the time, but we also know that the problems will get solved. We know that because we've done it over and over. We know we can depend on each other."

Employees often describe Safe Flight as "a feet-first company," meaning the only way anybody goes out the door for good is feet first. There is no mandatory retirement age. People are welcome to work as long as they want to work, and if a veteran employee wants to cut back to part-time, the company attempts to tailor a new schedule for him or her.

"Nobody leaves," says Joe Gordon, the company's senior vice president of engineering. "Management has a very family-oriented philosophy, so once you're here and enjoying your work, you tend to embrace that philosophy. I've worked with some people here for more than 30 years. They know my family, and I've watched their kids grow up. My kids have been here for our events, and then my grandkids started coming. That makes for a very special kind of camaraderie you just don't find at larger companies anymore."

THE ICE PROBLEM

Icing has always been a critical problem for pilots, adding weight to an aircraft, disrupting the flow of air around the wings, and presenting one of aviation's most problematic flight conditions. As engineer Paul Levine remembers, the idea for a new type of ice-detection system—one that paradoxically employs 170-year-old technology—came about as a number of Safe Flight employees were gathered in Leonard's office one day.

"I guess Len had read an accident report and decided this was something we could do something about," Levine says. "We knew there were a variety of ice detectors on the market, so our first thought was, 'What could we do that was different, that would be better than anything else already out there?'"

The most common ice detection system on the market uses a tuning-fork probe to alert a pilot to the existence of ice. When ice builds up on the tuning fork, its vibrational frequency changes, thereby warning the pilot that ice has begun to form on the airplane. The system is relatively heavy, expensive, and not readily applicable to smaller aircraft. Another competing system places a rotating shaft with ridges on the outside of the fuselage; when the shaft turns, it sends an electrical current to a sensor inside the plane. A buildup of ice in the ridges keeps the shaft from rotating; a current detector notes that the shaft has stopped turning and tells the pilot that ice is building up. Whatever their benefits and disadvantages, both of those systems have one crucial drawback in common: they don't warn a pilot until *after* ice has begun forming on the aircraft.

Safe Flight set out to build something that would warn pilots of the danger *before* ice started forming. Paul Levine developed a sensor that identifies the presence of moisture at specific temperatures—and by calibrating that sensor to sound an alert as the ice begins to form, Safe Flight created the first advance ice warning system.

Levine's solution was based on the principle of the refraction of light through a prism. He took a prism with known angles of refraction and exposed it to the air. Whatever moisture was in the air collected on the prism, changing its refraction index. Information, based on the new refraction index, about the amount of moisture present in the air was then combined with air temperature data to warn the pilot of the icing condition. This refraction principle had been used in the 1830s to gauge the amount of oil remaining in a lamp. Levine built a sensor, and the prototype was complete.

Safe Flight tested its new Ice Warning System in flight on its own Beech B55 Baron and then took the prototype into the Canadian Icing Research Centre wind tunnel in Ottawa to measure its performance against the FAA's standard for ice detection. Tom Grunbeck, Safe Flight's senior vice president of sales and marketing, says the company's sensor "can detect ice within half a second, while the best product currently on the market will take up to a minute to alert the pilot. That minute can make a huge difference in the safety of the airplane, enabling a pilot to either get out of icing conditions or turn on the deicing equipment if the aircraft is so equipped." Not only is the Safe Flight Ice Warning System effective, according to Grunbeck, it costs 80 percent less and is a fraction of the weight and power consumption of other products currently available.

SAFE FLIGHT'S ICE WARNING SYSTEM CAN BE MOUNTED ON AN AIRCRAFT'S WING OR TAIL. THE COMPANY DISPLAYED A TAIL-MOUNTED DEVICE, ABOVE, WHEN IT INTRODUCED THE PRODUCT AT THE NATIONAL BUSINESS AIRCRAFT ASSOCIATION CONVENTION IN 2007. OPPOSITE, THE GROUND CREW DEICES A BOEING 737 AT FRANCE'S ROISSY AIRPORT.

SAFE FLIGHT'S ORIGINAL LIFT INSTRUMENTATION SYSTEMS DEMONSTRATED A CRITICAL NEED FOR LIFT AND ANGLE OF ATTACK SENSING DURING LOW-SPEED PHASES OF FLIGHT, AND ITS STALL WARNING SYSTEMS WERE EMBRACED BY THE ENTIRE AVIATION INDUSTRY. SAFE FLIGHT PRODUCTS ARE NOW FOUND ON TWO-THIRDS OF THE ESTIMATED 40,000 PLANES CURRENTLY IN USE, AND ITS WING LIFT SENSORS ARE ON ALL AIRCRAFT PRODUCED BY DIAMOND AVIATION. THE TURBO DIESEL-POWERED DIAMOND DA42 TWIN STAR, SEEN HERE, IS SAFE FLIGHT-EQUIPPED.

NEW ANGLE OF ATTACK SYSTEMS

As Safe Flight looks ahead, its ambitions are for continual growth—not for size alone but for the promise of a future in which a steady introduction of new products is balanced by the continuous enhancement of existing products and the search for new applications for proven systems.

New applications are still being found for Safe Flight's oldest product lines: wing lift detectors and transducers, and fuselage airflow sensors. "We're doing a lot of research into air sensor systems," Randall says. "The Chinese are building a new airliner, and we're making a very advanced angle of attack system for that. In Brazil, Embraer is building new small business jets, and we're doing the angle of attack systems for them." The Chinese ARJ21 regional commercial jetliner is scheduled to make its first flight in 2008. The Brazilian aircraft maker Embraer has been working on two new planes—both small executive or corporate jets—that entered flight tests in 2007 and 2008.

Randall says Safe Flight's newest angle of attack systems are being developed to

MAKING
WATER BOMBING
SAFER

In the early 1990s a Canadian firefighting company came to Safe Flight with a unique lift measurement problem. The company had converted a fleet of Convair 580s into water bombers, which carry water in huge tanks to drop on forest fires and other large blazes.

After the conversion, the planes encountered an unexpected problem—accidents. Because water bombers have to drop their cargo—which weighs tons—in an instant, the planes undergo a dramatic change in gross weight, and thus angle of attack. To compensate, pilots would either climb too quickly, pulling too much vertical acceleration, or, conversely, not climb quickly enough and thus risk flying into the ground. Simply knowing their airspeed did the pilots no good, since the proper airspeed for a pullout would differ drastically before and after the cargo drop.

The solution to the company's problem lay in Safe Flight's core technology; the company built an angle of attack sensor for the Convair. As Senior Design Engineer Ray Bloch explains, "The pilots knew to fly within a certain range on that indicator and just within that range. Whether they had a full load of water or no water at all, they just had to fly the proper angle of attack and they were fine."

THIS ANGLE OF ATTACK SENSOR,

HERE SHOWN RESTING ON THE

BLUEPRINTS FOR ITS DESIGN,

ENABLES FIREFIGHTING WATER

BOMBERS TO REMAIN SAFELY

AIRBORNE AFTER UNDERGOING

A MASSIVE WEIGHT LOSS WHEN

DROPPING THEIR LOADS. OPPOSITE,

A CONVAIR 580 RELEASES WATER

OVER A WILDFIRE IN PORTUGAL

IN 2003.

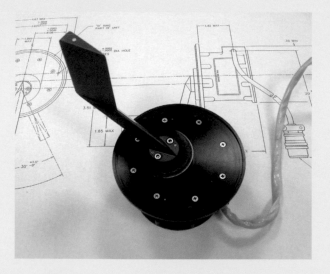

SAFE FLIGHT'S ANGLE OF ATTACK SENSOR IS NOW AN EXTREMELY SOPHISTICATED SYSTEM THAT PROVIDES PILOTS OF A VARIETY OF AIRPLANES, INCLUDING THE CESSNA CITATION CJ2+, SHOWN LEFT IN PRODUCTION IN WICHITA, KANSAS, WITH AN INCREASING AMOUNT OF FLIGHT-CRITICAL DATA. SAFE FLIGHT PRODUCT SUPPORT ENGINEER CHRIS WITHERS, FOREGROUND, RIGHT, SHOWS CIRRUS DESIGN MECHANICAL ENGINEER JIM SCHAFF A LIFT TRANSDUCER INSTALLED ON A CIRRUS DESIGN PROTOTYPE AIRCRAFT. BELOW, AN AD FOR SAFE FLIGHT'S INTEGRATED AOA SYSTEM.

provide more data from more sensors and to incorporate new features and modifications to improve performance and lower cost. One version adds a Pitot tube—a fluid flow velocity meter that provides data on air pressure and thus airspeed—to an airflow sensor. "That'll give a pilot Pitot pressure, in addition to the angle of attack, and we're developing that specifically for use on the new composite aircraft that have highly smooth skins," he says. He also says the company is developing an angle of attack probe with a servo motor to move the transducer probe to its full range for ground testing.

"That has some very good safety implications," Randall says. "Normally, the angle of attack data, the Pitot pressure, and static pressure are all fed into an air data computer that provides the needed information to a variety of systems. We're developing an angle of attack probe that does all that. Our airflow angle sensor will include air data computation, a big expansion of the information the angle of attack sensor has traditionally provided, with the benefit of greatly reduced power, weight, volume, and expense."

MORE THAN A HALF-MILLION SAFE FLIGHT STALL WARNING AND/OR ANGLE OF ATTACK SYSTEMS HAVE BEEN INSTALLED ON MORE THAN 400 DIFFERENT AIRCRAFT TYPES SINCE 1946. ONE OF THE FIRST LIFT DETECTORS WAS CERTIFIED ON A BEECHCRAFT, AND SINCE THAT TIME SAFE FLIGHT PRODUCTS HAVE BEEN USED CONTINUOUSLY ON BEECHCRAFT AIRPLANES, INCLUDING THE HAWKER-BEECHCRAFT KING AIR C90GTI, LEFT. SAFE FLIGHT'S RELATION-SHIP WITH PIPER GOES BACK ALMOST AS LONG, AND THE MAJORITY OF PIPER'S MODELS HAVE BEEN EQUIPPED WITH SAFE FLIGHT LIFT DETECTORS AND TRANSDUCERS, INCLUDING THE SINGLE-ENGINE MERIDIAN, OPPO-SITE BOTTOM. WHILE INITIALLY USED BY DOMESTIC MANUFAC-TURERS, SAFE FLIGHT PRODUCTS ARE NOW INSTALLED BY MANU-FACTURERS AROUND THE WORLD. AMONG THEM IS ITALY'S ALENIA AERMACCHI, KNOWN FOR ITS MILITARY TRAINING AIRCRAFT LIKE THE TWO AEROBATIC SF-260Es, OPPOSITE TOP.

It has been predicted that the number of helicopters in active service will double in the near future. For companies like Safe Flight, helicopters represent a major opportunity to do for helicopter flight what Safe Flight has done for fixed-wing aircraft since the 1940s.

PROJECT ENGINEER PAUL LEVINE
AND CO-OP STUDENT LOUIS
SIMONS CHECK THE ANTENNA
PLACEMENT OF SAFE FLIGHT'S
POWERLINE DETECTION SYSTEM
BEFORE A TEST FLIGHT IN A BELL
205 (HUEY). THE PRODUCT CAME
INTO BEING WHEN RANDALL
GREENE READ ABOUT AN ACCIDENT
IN WHICH A RESCUE HELICOPTER
HIT POWERLINES AND CRASHED.
HELICOPTERS, SUCH AS THE ONE
OPPOSITE ON A COMMUTE TO
WALL STREET, OFTEN OPERATE IN
CLOSE PROXIMITY TO POWERLINES
AND OTHER HAZARDOUS WIRES.

MAKING CHOPPERS SAFER

Over its first half-century, Safe Flight made products almost exclusively for fixed-wing aircraft, but in recent years the company has begun development of safety systems to meet the growing needs of helicopters and even gliders.

The helicopter has been described, supposedly in jest, as an assembly of 40,000 loose pieces flying more or less in formation. "There is a substantial difference between fixed-wing aircraft and helicopters," says Randall Greene, who has spent much of his career flying helicopters. In addition to his qualifications on numerous fixed-wing aircraft, he's flown flight tests on the 1950s Hiller YH32A with a hybrid augmented ramjet of Safe Flight's design. He also is an FAA Designated Engineering Representative test pilot for FAR Part 23 and 25 airplanes and Part 27 and 29 helicopters.

"Fixed-wing aircraft have positive stability," Randall says. "In a certain sense, they know how to fly, and they even seem to enjoy it. When I'm teaching somebody to fly an airplane, I half-jokingly say to them, 'You need to tell it where you want to get it to go, but basically it wants to do the flying itself.' But helicopters are different. To emphasize the lack of positive stability, I tell students that if you let go of a helicopter, it will try to kill you. That's really the first thing it wants to do when it gets up in the morning."

The helicopter business is one of the fastest-growing sectors in the aviation industry. In 2006 more than 26,000 helicopters were in civilian service, and many thousands more were in use by the military. It has been predicted that the number of helicopters in active service will double in the near future. For companies like Safe Flight, helicopters represent a potentially huge market for new products.

One of the most serious hazards faced by helicopter pilots is presented by powerlines. Between 1997 and 2006, more than 50 U.S. Army helicopters struck powerlines, resulting in 13 deaths and millions of dollars in damage. During that same period the National Transportation Safety Board reported 102 civilian helicopter wire strikes and 33 deaths. For Randall, the need for a reliable powerline warning was made clear one foggy day when he was living in Colorado.

"There had been a horrific car accident, and the first responders called for a helicopter to medevac the victims out of there. The helicopter landed on the road, right next to some powerlines. It took them more than 45 minutes to get one of the victims out of the car and into the helicopter. Having forgotten about them, the pilot took off

and flew right into the powerlines he'd landed next to. They were all killed."

In 1999 Randall suggested that Safe Flight try to develop a powerline detector. Several detectors were on the market, but they seemed impractical to him. As he points out, "There's a laser device, but it costs something like $250,000 and weighs 30-some pounds, so it's very heavy for a helicopter. The most popular device currently in use, believe it or not, is a set of wire cutters. They put these blades on the top and bottom of the cabin—based on the theory that, if you inadvertently fly into wires, the device will cut them."

Randall says that although he's never heard of the wire-cutting system actually saving anyone's life, he believes the fact that such a device even exists makes the point: "There is a need for something to keep helicopters out of wires." Clearly, the market existed. The challenge was inventing a warning system that was lightweight enough for a helicopter, reliable, and reasonably inexpensive. He noted that powerlines generate an electromagnetic field, and the field will interfere with radio signals. If you drive your car toward a powerline, the electromagnetic field will cause static on the AM radio frequencies, and the static will grow louder as the car gets closer to the line. This fact formed the nucleus of Safe Flight's first product for helicopters.

Randall Greene postulated that RF (radio frequency) could be the answer, and he had Safe Flight engineers build a radio device sensitive to 60Hz, the frequency of the field emitted by commercial powerlines in the United States. Again, it was Paul Levine who came up with the solution. He found an inexpensive radio that astronomy clubs often use to listen for radio signals from space. Randall attached a portable antenna to a helicopter and took a test flight. It worked, in principle. Randall began by experimenting with a simple RF detection device, driving around Boulder, Colorado, in his car to prove the theory. It worked in the car. He then put one in a helicopter, but he quickly discovered

SAFE FLIGHT'S POWERLINE DETECTION SYSTEM, SHOWN IN OPERATION DURING A 2007 TEST FLIGHT IN THE COMPANY'S BELL 206B, HELPS HELICOPTER PILOTS AVOID CONTACT WITH POWERLINES. A LOW FREQUENCY RECEIVER SCANS FOR THE PRESENCE OF AN ELECTROMAGNETIC FIELD GENERATED BY A POWERLINE. WHEN THE SYSTEM DETECTS SUCH A FIELD, THE RED LIGHT SEEN HERE ON THE INSTRUMENT PANEL IS ILLUMINATED, AND A PERSISTENT AUDIO SIGNAL BEGINS CLICKING. THE LIGHT REMAINS LIT AND THE SIGNAL CONTINUES UNTIL THE DANGER HAS PASSED. AS A SAFE FLIGHT ADVERTISEMENT FOR THE PRODUCT, OPPOSITE, NOTES, COMPETING SYSTEMS USE EXPENSIVE WIRE CUTTERS THAT PILOTS CAN USE IN A HIGH-RISK BID TO CUT THEIR WAY THROUGH CONTACT WITH POWERLINES.

during testing that the device had to be coupled to the proper antenna design to provide an orientation that would be effective for a moving aircraft.

Inventing the core powerline detection technology was relatively simple. Turning it into a product was another matter—and it took almost four years to solve complex antenna and signal-orientation issues before the FAA could certify the initial 60Hz version of the system, which was STC'd in 2005. EASA, the European Aviation Safety Agency, certified Safe Flight's 50Hz device in 2007.

Norm Rosenblum, Safe Flight's manager of international contracts, says the company's powerline detector is substantially less expensive than other warning systems on the market. "We've sold the device all over the world, from Canada to Russia to Australia," he says. "The oddest request we've ever had was at a helicopter show in England. I was approached by a man who wanted to buy a system right there. He wanted to carry it home. It turned out he didn't even own a helicopter. He wanted to put it in his limousine to alert him when he was driving near a downed powerline."

HELICOPTER EXCEEDANCE WARNING

Because helicopters fly at low altitudes, hover in position for extended periods, and often operate in densely populated areas, chopper pilots fly "eyes outside" their aircraft, meaning their attention is focused on everything happening around them. They continually scan the skies even in priority over checking cockpit instruments.

It can be easy for a helicopter pilot to unwittingly exceed the operating limit of the engine—to use too much torque or exceed the engine's thermal limits, potentially causing serious engine damage. Sometimes a pilot has no option but to push engine limits to complete a mission, but in most cases "over-temping" an engine is an oversight as a pilot maintains focus on his external surroundings. Often a pilot is never aware that an engine limit has been exceeded, and the helicopter exhibits no immediate symptoms.

Taking advantage of the same stick shaker warning technology that the company pioneered for fixed-wing aircraft, Safe Flight developed its Exceedance Warning System to alert pilots to an over-temp or over-torque condition. The system uses a stick shaker mounted on the collective (the cockpit control with which the pilot controls rotor pitch and engine thrust), driven by a Safe Flight exceedance monitor computer to warn a pilot

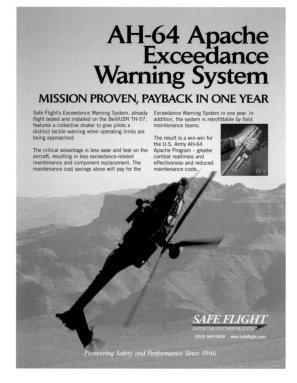

SAFE FLIGHT CO-OP STUDENT LOUIS SIMONS, OPPOSITE, SETS UP DIAGNOSTIC AND FLIGHT TEST EQUIPMENT FOR A NEW POWERLINE DETECTION SYSTEM UNDER DEVELOPMENT. SAFE FLIGHT IS DEVELOPING AN INCREASING NUMBER OF PRODUCTS FOR HELICOPTERS, INCLUDING, AS ADVERTISED ABOVE, AN EXCEEDANCE WARNING SYSTEM THAT TELLS PILOTS WHEN THEIR AIRCRAFT EXCEED CRITICAL ENGINE TEMPERATURE AND TORQUE THRESHOLDS.

SAFE FLIGHT IS THE LEADING SUPPLIER OF WING LIFT TECHNOLOGY TO THE AVIATION INDUSTRY. ITS THIRD-GENERATION SPEED CONTROL SYSTEM PROVIDES PILOTS WITH LIFT INFORMATION TO OPTIMIZE THEIR AIRCRAFT'S PERFORMANCE. THE CONTINUOUS COCKPIT DISPLAY ENABLES A PILOT TO INSTANTLY EVALUATE LIFT PERFORMANCE REGARDLESS OF GROSS WEIGHT, WING LOADING, AIR DENSITY, ATTITUDE, GROUND EFFECT, TURBULENCE, OR FLAP/GEAR CONFIGURATION—PARTICULARLY VALUABLE IN AIRCRAFT LIKE AVIAT AIRCRAFT'S HUSKY, RIGHT, WHICH IS MADE FOR "FLYING INTO PLACES OTHER PLANES SIMPLY CAN'T," AND QUEST AIRCRAFT'S NEW KODIAK, OPPOSITE TOP, WHICH WAS DEVELOPED SPECIFICALLY FOR USE BY MISSIONARIES IN DEVELOPING COUNTRIES. THE CESSNA 400, OPPOSITE BOTTOM, THE INDUSTRY'S FASTEST FOUR-PASSENGER, SINGLE-ENGINE PISTON PRODUCTION AIRCRAFT, ALSO CARRIES SAFE FLIGHT SYSTEMS.

that the helicopter is approaching engine temperature or torque or rotor mast torque limits. In 2003 the Exceedance Warning System was FAA/STC-certified on the Bell 206B JetRanger and installed on the Navy's TH57 fleet, its training helicopter. Based on the success of the Navy program, the Army has made the warning system required equipment on its entire fleet of more than 700 AH64 Apaches.

Whereas Safe Flight's Exceedance Warning System provides real-time feedback to the pilot, enabling the pilot to take preventive action, the only competing system on the market works only after the flight, analyzing downloaded data to determine what maintenance needs to be performed on the helicopter.

RANDALL GREENE AND FORMER SAFE FLIGHT AERODYNAMICIST SHARON NETHERCROFT EXAMINE THE WING OF A CIRRUS SR22 TO DETERMINE THE BEST PLACEMENT FOR THE LIFT TRANSDUCER. SAFE FLIGHT IS WORKING WITH CIRRUS ON A SYSTEM THAT WILL GIVE PILOTS PRE-STALL WARNING AND LOW AIRSPEED AWARENESS INFORMATION.

SOARING SAFELY

Another area of aviation that Safe Flight has begun to explore is the world of soaring, gliding through the skies without engines. Stall spin accidents are a major concern for glider pilots, and they could benefit from a reliable angle of attack system that could tell them if their craft was in danger of stalling.

The challenge in developing such a system for soaring is that gliders, with their smooth wings and fuselages, are extraordinarily drag-sensitive—and adding anything to the outside can significantly affect the plane's performance. Furthermore, gliders don't produce electric power, so any system on the plane has to operate on very little power.

Safe Flight again adapted existing technology—in this case, developed for one of Leonard's passions, sailboat racing—to solve the problem. Back in the 1980s, he had invented and briefly marketed several products for sailboats. One of these was an angle of attack system that used a

Safety First
Angle-of-Attack/Stall Warning

Deadly stall-spin events at low altitude are far less likely with Safe Flight's Angle-of-Attack/Stall Warning system.

Flying at high wing loading, it is difficult for pilots to notice if they are thermalling too slowly. As a result, it is easy to thermal out of the "sweet spot" or best performance point on the drag polar. As the bank angle increases, the required increase in airspeed increases. Safe Flight's Angle of Attack/Stall Warning system aids the pilot in identifying and avoiding loss of high drag performance.

The system weighs less than one pound, is easily installed and requires very little power.

ANGLE OF ATTACK

SAFE FLIGHT
INSTRUMENT CORPORATION
(914) 946-9500 www.safeflight.com
Pioneering Safety and Performance Since 1946

CORPORATE ANGEL NETWORK

Leonard Greene received a phone call in 1981 from a woman named Pat Blum, a writer, commercial pilot, and cancer survivor, who wanted to propose an idea. A resident of Greenwich, Connecticut, not far from the Westchester County Airport in White Plains, New York, she had noticed how frequently corporate aircraft took off and headed to all parts of the country carrying only a few passengers. That seemed to her like a valuable opportunity to address the vital transportation needs of cancer patients.

Blum had learned, while battling her own cancer, how expensive it can be for a patient to travel around the country to get specialized medical treatment. While health insurance covers many medical bills, it does not cover most of the incidental costs, including transportation, lodging, and food. These items can cost thousands of dollars and are often beyond the financial resources of many cancer patients. Her concept was a simple one: allow cancer patients who need transportation to use the empty seats on corporate aircraft at no charge.

"I thought those planes could be like magic carpets," she recalls. "They could give corporations a unique means of combining business activities with demonstrated social responsibility."

It turns out that Leonard was the perfect person for Blum to call with her idea. His second wife, Phyllis, had died of cancer in 1965, and he was very much aware of the difficulties cancer patients face. Leonard joined Blum and her friend Jay Weinberg—himself a two-time cancer survivor—to become cofounders of the Corporate Angel Network (CAN). Not only did Greene offer CAN the use of Safe Flight's plane, he piloted the first Corporate Angel Network flight, from White Plains to Detroit, bringing a 19-year-old boy home for Christmas. Later he piloted the 100th flight, the 1,000th flight, and, with his son Randall as his copilot, the 10,000th flight.

IN JANUARY 2008 A SIX-YEAR-OLD PATIENT NAMED NATALIE, SEEN HERE WITH HER MOTHER, WAS FLOWN HOME TO FLORIDA ON A PEPSICO CORPORATE JET AFTER BEING TREATED FOR NEUROBLASTOMA, A CHILDHOOD CANCER, AT NEW YORK'S MEMORIAL SLOAN-KETTERING CANCER CENTER. NATALIE FLEW AS CAN'S 25,000TH PATIENT.

CAN meant a lot to Leonard. "As a human being, it makes you feel good if you can give a helping hand," he said. "Truthfully, it's also good for our image, because helping cancer patients paints a very different picture of businessmen than the usual image of them being interested only in making money or destroying the environment or making poor people poorer." CAN is an important Safe Flight and Greene family interest. Before moving to its own offices at Westchester County Airport, CAN operated out of donated office space in Safe Flight's building. Leonard's daughter, Bonnie LeVar, currently serves as CAN's president. Randall Greene is chairman of the board, one comprised of leaders of the aerospace industry—among them the CEOs of Cessna, Dassault Falcon Jet, and Hawker Beechcraft.

Gulfstream Aerospace, a longtime Safe Flight customer, was also one of the first companies to become a corporate angel. Its president, Joe Lombardo, says his company is "extremely proud to have been a member of CAN for more than 25 years. In fact, to acknowledge and celebrate our 25th anniversary of working with CAN, we put a special logo on all of our demonstrator aircraft."

Corporate Angel Network has succeeded beyond the cofounders' wildest dreams. Since its founding, more than 550 corporations, including most of the *Fortune* 100, have provided more than 28,000 flights. In May 1984 President Ronald Reagan bestowed the Volunteer in Action award, the highest honor the United States can bestow on a volunteer program, on CAN.

There is no way to estimate the amount of money the Corporate Angel Network has saved cancer patients since its founding, but its value is measured in far more than those savings. It's a stress-free blessing for patients and their families, as well as for corporations and their executives, who have the opportunity to offer outreach to others in need.

transducer mounted on the underside of the hull to measure the leeway angle, the amount of leeward drift of a boat as it tacks through the water. Leonard and Safe Flight's engineers had designed the transducer for the famed *Courageous*, the 12-meter yacht that Leonard purchased and entered in the 1983 America's Cup trials.

Since sailboats' electronic systems run on batteries, Safe Flight developed a transducer that required minimal power. Engineer Pete Cordes, who had worked on the *Courageous* project to help adapt the transducer for gliders, also developed an extraordinarily low-drag airflow vane. The device looks a bit like a dinner knife sticking out of the side of the fuselage.

Safe Flight installed the system on its Schempp-Hirth Duo Discus, a two-seat glider, in 2006. Soaring enthusiasts received the initial system well and fed back valuable information that has helped Safe Flight develop the system's second generation, which is installed on the company's single-seat Schempp-Hirth Discus 2c glider. Because gliders fly close to stall conditions much of the time, pilots wanted a system that would alert them before the stall but not generate nuisance warnings. Again, Safe Flight met that

SENIOR VICE PRESIDENT OF SALES AND MARKETING TOM GRUNBECK HAS WELCOMED VISITORS TO SAFE FLIGHT'S TRADE SHOW BOOTH, SUCH AS THE ONE, LEFT, AT THE 2007 NATIONAL BUSINESS AIR-CRAFT ASSOCIATION CONVENTION, SINCE HE JOINED THE COMPANY IN 2003. SINCE HIS ARRIVAL, IN ADDITION TO ITS TRADITIONAL PRODUCTS FOR FIXED-WING POWERED FLIGHT, THE COMPANY HAS DEVELOPED A RANGE OF NEW PRODUCTS FOR HELICOPTERS AND GLIDERS.

challenge, and the new Angle of Attack/Stall Warning System was introduced to the soaring community in 2007.

IMPERMANENCE AND ENDURANCE

Leonard Greene died, at the age of 88, in November 2006 without seeing the introduction of the glider device born of his love of sailing. In 55 years at the helm of his company, he had invented important life-saving devices now commonplace on most of the world's aircraft. With boundless energy and passion, he never stopped inventing—and working to keep Safe Flight unique.

Joe Wilson, Safe Flight's chief operating officer, joined the company in 2001. He was drawn to Safe Flight largely because of what Leonard had created: a "company that felt like family" and one that could "react very quickly to the needs of the marketplace and, frankly, outmaneuver our competitors." As for Leonard himself, Wilson says, "Almost until his death, he was still coming up with ideas, still having engineering meetings, still assisting in development projects, still actively engaged."

"Len's forte was creativity," recalls Robert Teter. "We don't want to ever lose that.

SAFE FLIGHT'S RELATIONSHIP WITH GULFSTREAM AEROSPACE DATES TO THE EARLY 1950s. GULFSTREAM PRESIDENT EMERITUS BRYAN T. MOSS SAYS THAT "FROM THE START THERE WERE TECHNICAL CAPABILITIES AND A WORK ATTITUDE THAT APPEALED TO GULFSTREAM." CURRENT GULFSTREAM PRESIDENT JOE LOMBARDO ADDS, "WE HAVE AN INSTALLED FLEET OF 1,500 AIRPLANES, AND [SAFE FLIGHT IS] ON EVERY ONE OF OUR MODELS." THEY INCLUDE THE G200 ATS PICTURED HERE AND THE LARGE-CABIN GULFSTREAM BEING MANUFACTURED, OPPOSITE TOP. OPPOSITE BOTTOM, SENIOR MECHANICAL ENGINEER JACK STEINER CONDUCTS A PROTOTYPE FIT CHECK FOR SAFE FLIGHT'S AUTOPOWER SYSTEM ON THE GULFSTREAM G150.

"When customers buy one of our products, they know reliability and safety are part of our history. So when we buy products from Safe Flight, they have to meet a very high standard to fulfill our customers' expectations."

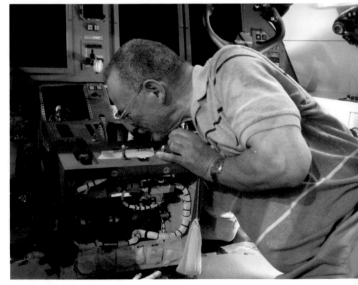

—Joe Lombardo, President, Gulfstream Aerospace

SAFE FLIGHT'S ELECTROMAGNETIC INTERFERENCE (EMI) TEST CHAMBER ENABLES ENGINEERS TO TEST PRODUCTS TO ENSURE COMPLIANCE WITH THE CERTIFICATION STANDARDS FOR INSTALLATION AND USE ON AIRCRAFT. THE CHAMBER AND ASSOCIATED EQUIPMENT CAN TEST FOR RADIATED EMISSIONS AND TEST THE SUSCEPTIBILITY OF ELECTRONICS TO RADIO FRE-QUENCY INTERFERENCE AND HIGH-ENERGY SURGES RESULTING FROM LIGHTNING STRIKES TO AN AIRCRAFT. THE CHAMBER IS AN IMPORTANT DESIGN TOOL THAT ALLOWS ENGINEERS TO TEST ELEMENTS OF A DESIGN BEFORE FULLY ASSEMBLING PROTOTYPE EQUIPMENT—GIVING SAFE FLIGHT HIGH CONFIDENCE THAT FINAL DESIGNS WILL MEET STANDARDS WHILE ALSO MEETING A PRO-GRAM'S COST TARGETS AND DEADLINES. HERE, MICHAEL BOCCHINFUSO READIES THE TEST EQUIPMENT IN THE CHAMBER, WHICH WAS INSTALLED IN 2008.

That's certainly one of the hallmarks of Safe Flight, but the industry has changed drastically since he founded this company. Our corporate culture is still the way it has always been, but we've made major investments in our infrastructure."

The search for and development of new products at Safe Flight remains constant. As has been the case so many times in the past, new concepts are coming from experience. For example, when Randall was aloft one night in Safe Flight's Bell 206 helicopter, he discovered that both landing lights had burned out—a potential problem as he flew into the night. He'd already walked away from one engine-out helicopter night landing—and one night autorotation seemed like a good number not to exceed. From that experience Safe Flight developed the Landing Light Status Annunciator, a warning light that will alert the pilot if one or both of the landing light filaments are burned out—even if a landing light has not been turned on.

New product concepts also come directly from articulated needs of the industry. Safe Flight's sales staff is constantly in the field, talking to longtime customers and prospects to understand their problems, needs, and safety concerns.

"Sometimes we think we're like custom tailors," says Ray Bloch. "Can you make the sleeves a little longer? Can you make something for us that'll do this? Once, we had a customer who wanted an angle of attack system for an airplane with a peculiarity.

Normally, airplanes have a wing flap position selector handle that stops at certain points, called detents. This was the first airplane we'd seen that didn't have any detents. We had to develop a normalized (flap-compensated) angle of attack system that would be good for any position at which the flaps were set. We do things like that all the time."

What has made Safe Flight successful is the ability to continually develop new products and adapt existing technologies to the entire field of aviation, while providing extraordinary support to its customers—

"WE'VE BROUGHT SAFE FLIGHT FROM THE PAPER WORLD INTO THE DIGITAL WORLD," EXPLAINS COMPUTER AIDED DESIGN OPERATOR DEMETRIUS ALPHONSO, ABOVE, AT RIGHT. HERE HE AND VICE PRESIDENT OF RESEARCH AND DEVELOPMENT BOB TETER EXAMINE A LIFT TRANSDUCER FOR THE CIRRUS SR22. JOE WILSON, LEFT, JOINED SAFE FLIGHT AS EXECUTIVE VICE PRESIDENT IN 2001 AND WAS PROMOTED TO CHIEF OPERATING OFFICER IN 2008. "WHEN I WALKED THROUGH THE FRONT DOOR, I SAW THIS WAS NOT AT ALL THE TYPICAL AEROSPACE COMPANY," HE SAYS.

SAFE FLIGHT ADAPTED TECHNOLOGY IT HAD DEVELOPED FOR OFFSHORE SAILBOAT RACING TO PRODUCE A LOW-DRAG AIRFLOW VANE FOR GLIDERS SUCH AS THE ONE AT LEFT. WHEN UNEXPECTED CHALLENGES AROSE DURING TESTING OF EMBRAER'S NEW PHENOM 100, EMBRAER TURNED TO SAFE FLIGHT TO DEVELOP SPECIALIZED PRODUCTS—INCLUDING A UNIQUE HEATER MONITORING SYSTEM. THEY WERE FLIGHT-TESTED BY A TRIO OF EMBRAER PILOTS, BELOW LEFT. IN 2008 SAFE FLIGHT WON AN EMBRAER BEST SUPPLIERS AWARD, BELOW, FOR DEVELOPMENT EXCELLENCE ON THE PHENOM 100 PROGRAM.

with response times and a level of continuity large corporations can't match. Perhaps nothing better illustrates this than a contract Embraer awarded in late 2007.

Safe Flight has been a supplier to the Brazilian aircraft maker for more than three decades, but as Embraer in the 1990s turned to integrators for complete avionics suites for new airplanes, Safe Flight found itself relegated to providing limited components in other vendors' systems. "We literally got knocked off the jets," says Norm Rosenblum. But, he says, Safe Flight continued to enthusiastically support, update, and enhance its products on older Embraer planes.

When Embraer initially awarded contracts for its new Phenom 100 executive jet, the avionics suite went to a large integrator. Safe Flight received a contract to supply only the angle of attack sensor for a competitor's stall warning system.

Because of Safe Flight's technical expertise in stall warning and its years of quality support to Embraer, the aircraft maker revised its contracts in December 2007 and made Safe Flight the exclusive supplier of the entire stall warning system. Moreover, Embraer also awarded Safe Flight a contract to provide the company's innovative heater monitoring system for the Phenom 100's air data and angle of attack probes—a new product

that Safe Flight developed as an outgrowth of its Helicopter Landing Light Status Annunciator.

It's with this kind of dedication and pride that the people of Safe Flight turn their customers' challenges into products that save lives and improve aircraft performance. As Production Manager Greg Tassio explains, "When I get on an airplane, I always look to see our products. I think we all do that. I remember the last time I flew out of Westchester County Airport. As I got on the aircraft, a 21-passenger Embraer turboprop, I looked at the fuselage. There was one of our airflow angle sensors. Because my area of the factory did most of the production, I was quite certain I had built it. So I said to the person next to me, 'Oh look, there's an 85107.' It didn't mean anything to him, but to me it represented my whole career. And it gave me a great deal of satisfaction."

Such spirit, attention to detail, knowledge, and experience have kept Safe Flight Instrument Corporation a tiny leader among giants—ever since Leonard Greene set out to solve a single problem and ended up creating one of the most enduring companies in the aviation industry. As Leonard said many times and as his son echoes today, even as the company continues its steady growth: being big has never held appeal for Safe Flight, and that's not likely to change.

"Expansion isn't our objective," Randall says. "We don't intend to grow just to get bigger; we intend to get better at those things we've been doing successfully for more than 60 years." That said, however, Safe Flight's sales have more than doubled over the past five years—and, as Safe Flight looks ahead, it spies a future as the lean, innovative problem solver it has been for six decades, tightly integrated as ever with its customers.

As Cessna's Jack Pelton, whose entire fleet carries Safe Flight products, says, "Safe Flight is in our corporate DNA. It's kind of a given that they will be on our future programs."

Such spirit, attention to detail, knowledge, and experience have kept Safe Flight Instrument Corporation a tiny leader among giants—ever since Leonard Greene set out to solve a single problem and ended up creating one of the most enduring companies in the aviation industry.

Acknowledgments

I would like to gratefully acknowledge the assistance of every member of the Safe Flight staff from whom I requested even the slightest assistance. I have rarely seen so many people so willing to give of their time with such enthusiasm. In particular, I would like to thank Matt Greene for his always good-natured and rapid response to even my most complex questions. I would also like to mention that being privileged to spend many hours with Leonard Greene— then nearer than any of us knew to the end of his life—was a rare treat.

Of course, I would also like to acknowledge my wife, Laura, who was there to provide love and support from early morning to those very late nights.

—David Fisher, December 2008

PHOTO CREDITS:

Cover and page 3 © Premium Stock/CORBIS
Page 4-5 © B.S.P.I./CORBIS
Pages 7, 59, 83, 85, 90(upper left), 91, 98(lower left), 117(upper right), 118(both), 119, 122, 123(both), 125(both) and 133(all) © Edwina Stevenson
Page 8-9 © John McAnulty/CORBIS
Page 10-11 © Frans Lanting/CORBIS
Pages 12, 18-19 and 30-31 © Museum of Flight/CORBIS
Page 42-43 appears courtesy of the Naval Historical Center
Pages 44-45 and 67 © Sunbird Photos by Don Boyd
Page 47 © Lake County Museum/CORBIS
Pages 50 and 104-105 appear courtesy of the Hawker Beechcraft Corporation
Pages 51, 82 and 88-89 appear courtesy of the U. S. Air Force
Page 52-53 and 74-75 appear courtesy of Bombardier Inc.
Page 56-57 appears courtesy of Yvonne Ahlers
Page 60 © Will & Deni McIntyre/CORBIS
Page 65 appears courtesy of the Institute for SocioEconomic Studies
Page 68-69 © Skyscan/CORBIS
Page 69 appears courtesy of Gary Weber
Page 78-79 © Richard Baker/CORBIS
Page 84 © 2008 Bill Bernstein
Page 87(both) appear courtesy of Peter Garrison

Pages 90(lower right), 95, 98(upper right), 101 (lower right), 107, 110, 115, 117(lower left) and 121(lower right) appear courtesy of Matt Greene
Page 92-93 appears courtesy of Bennet Greene
Page 94 © Annebicque Bernard/CORBIS SYGMA
Page 96-97 appears courtesy of Diamond Aircraft Industries Inc.
Page 100-101 appears courtesy of Tony Fishlock
Pages 102-103 and 113(lower) appear courtesy of the Cessna Aircraft Company
Page 104(upper) appears courtesy of Alenia Aermacchi
Pages 104(lower) and 112-113 © 2008 Breezeway
Page 106 © Russell Munson/CORBIS
Page 113(upper) appears courtesy of the Quest Aircraft Company
Page 116 appears courtesy of the Corporate Angel Network
Pages 120, 121(upper) appear courtesy of the Gulfstream Aerospace Corporation
Page 124(upper) © Ben Blankenburg/CORBIS
Page 124(lower left) appears courtesy of Embraer S.A.
Pages 126 and 126-127 © Charles O'Rear/CORBIS
Page 128-129 © Charles Krebs/CORBIS

All other photographs and historical items appear courtesy of Safe Flight Instrument Corporation.

Timeline

1937

During a flying lesson, Leonard Greene sees a plane suddenly stall and dive into the ground, killing the pilot. In response, he creates and tests a rudimentary stall warning system.

1943

While working as an engineer at Grumman during World War II, Greene writes a paper, *The Attenuation Method for Compressible Flow Systems*, which accurately predicts the physical consequences of breaking the sound barrier, and proposes a safe method for making it possible.

1946

Greene rents a barn on Russell Street in White Plains, New York, for $100 per month and establishes Safe Flight Instrument Corporation to market his $17 Stall Warning Indicator. He generates about $7,000 in revenue in his first year.

1947

The Saturday Evening Post praises the stall warning as "the greatest life saver since the invention of the parachute," and insurance companies begin offering a discount to owners who install it. Orders begin flowing in.

1948

Consolidated Vultee of Wayne, Michigan, becomes the first airplane manufacturer to make Safe Flight's stall warning system standard equipment on its new planes.

1949

Safe Flight adds a stick shaker to its Stall Warning Indicator. A large order from Grumman puts the company on solid financial footing.

Safe Flight is honored with the prestigious Flight Safety Foundation Air Safety Award.

1950

The growing company moves into the second floor of a large brick building on Water Street in White Plains.

1951

By replacing its original vane on the leading edge of the wing with an analog transducer, Safe Flight is able to measure a range of airflow positions, making possible many future innovations.

Safe Flight creates a manually flown speed control system for the Navy. A large order marks the beginning of a relationship between the company and the military that continues to flourish and grow.

1956

Safe Flight develops AutoPower, an automatic throttle system to control an aircraft's speed to a fixed angle of attack reference.

1958

The company introduces the Speed Command of Attitude and Thrust (SCAT) computer. This system provides a single display to help pilots make optimum takeoffs and landings. Within two years 24 airlines and the military have put it into regular service.

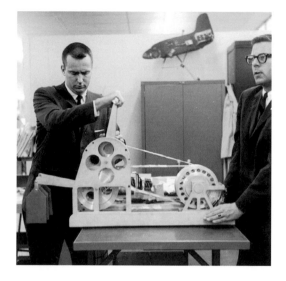

1964

Outgrowing its facilities, Safe Flight constructs and moves into a building on King Street in White Plains, adjoining the Westchester County Airport.

Safe Flight adds pilot-selected airspeed and Mach targets to its autothrottle system.

1967

Safe Flight briefly becomes a public company, and the stock trades as high as $66 per share. Deciding that he prefers a closely held company, Greene repurchases the stock and takes the company private again.

Safe Flight receives the Employer's Merit Award from New York State to honor its policy of hiring handicapped workers.

1972

Safe Flight begins marketing Wind Track, an autopilot system for sailboats. The product is ultimately discontinued, but basic ideas behind it are resurrected in the early 2000s when the company develops a stall warning system for glider aircraft.

1975

After a sudden wind shear causes an Eastern Airlines Boeing 727 to crash in New York, Greene invents a Wind Shear Warning System, and within a year United Airlines is testing it on Boeing 727 and 747 aircraft.

1979

Safe Flight receives FAA certification for its wind shear system on a Learjet 36A, the first of many business jets so certified.

Timeline

1980s	1990s	2000s

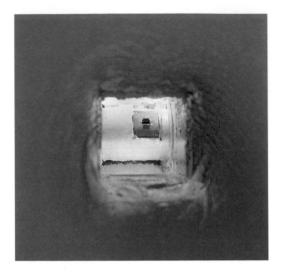

1981

Greene joins Pat Blum and Jay Weinberg to found the Corporate Angel Network to provide free air transportation to cancer patients and their families. Greene pilots the first flight in Safe Flight's plane; more than two decades later, he does the same for the 10,000th flight.

1982

Safe Flight receives the first of two consecutive Department of Defense Awards for Quality Excellence.

1991

Greene is inducted into the National Inventors Hall of Fame by Senator John Glenn.

1995

Randall Greene works with Safe Flight's engineers to create the N_1 Computer, a device that provides optimum thrust-setting information to pilots.

1999

Safe Flight begins developing a powerline detection system for helicopters. The product receives certification in the United States in 2005 and in Europe in 2007.

2001

Leonard Greene announces that his son Donald will succeed him as president of Safe Flight in 2002. But on September 11, Donald dies in a terrorist attack on United Airlines Flight 93. Randall takes the company helm and navigates Safe Flight through a perilous time period.

2003

Safe Flight receives its first certifications of a new Exceedance Warning System for helicopters, designed to warn a pilot when over-temperature or over-torque conditions are reached. The Navy puts the system on its TH57 training helicopters.

2004

Major interior and exterior renovation of Safe Flight's facility is begun.

2005

To demonstrate the efficiency of flying angle of attack, Randall Greene flies from White Plains to San Diego in Safe Flight's Falcon 20F, conserving sufficient fuel to make the nonstop flight in a record-setting six hours and 41 minutes.

2006

Leonard Greene dies at 88 years of age, having patented more than 100 inventions.

Safe Flight develops an Angle of Attack/Stall Warning System for use on gliders. It is introduced to the industry the following year.

2007

Safe Flight introduces an Ice Warning System that can detect and warn a pilot of ice buildup on an aircraft within a half-second of its formation.

Safe Flight begins development of new, advanced air sensor-based angle of attack systems designed to provide more data, improve performance, and lower cost.

2008

Safe Flight installs a new, state-of-the-art design laboratory and an electromagnetic interference test chamber—both intended to improve the company's ability to develop and test innovative products that meet program standards, costs, and schedules.

Chosen from among 120 suppliers to Embraer's Phenom 100 program, Safe Flight wins an Embraer Best Suppliers Award for excellence in many areas, including quality, on-time delivery, milestone achievement, engineering, cost, and flexibility.

Index

Bold listings indicate illustrations.